LAUREN COCHRANE

THE STORIES BEHIND
THE FASHION CLASSICS

WELBECK

CONTENTS

INTRODUCTION

EARLIER TODAY, I WENT for a walk. It was a nice day, in mid-September, so lots of people were out, enjoying the last vestiges of a London summer. This meant it was a great day for my favourite game, one I have been playing since I started writing this book. It's called outfit bingo – and involves counting how many I see of each item included here as I walk along. Today, in the short distance between my house and the local park, and back again, I spotted two biker jackets, six white T-shirts, one pair of ballet flats, four Breton tops, three miniskirts, one Little Black Dress, several hoodies, and lots and lots of jeans. The fact it was a weekend, and a fine day, would explain the lack of stilettos and trench coats.

I would be willing to bet that, much like the people on my walk, your outfit features at least one of these 10 items. I have certainly spent most of the time writing this book in a favourite pair of jeans and seen-better-days hoodie. The pieces selected here are unremarkable on purpose. Katie Holmes's bradigan and Billy Porter's amazing mechanical curtain hat for the Grammys (google it) are the fashion moments that go viral. But this is a book less about fashion and more about clothes. By focusing on the things we wear every day, we hold a mirror up to where we are at – and how we got here.

Take skinny jeans. Worn by punks in New York in the late 70s, they symbolized a conscious rejection of societal norms that still favoured flares. Fast-forward 40 years and the skinny jean is now the mainstream denim choice – accounting for 38 per cent of women's denim sales in 2020. The miniskirt's eyebrow-raising story, meanwhile, developed from the flappers of the 20s, through the 60s youthquake, evolving to Geri Halliwell's Union Jack "Girl Power" minidress in the 90s. Even today, the controversy of this item remains – and says much about the reality of gender politics now.

Respectable dressing on the disreputable:
William S Burroughs in a trench coat,
photographed by Allen Ginsberg

As we'll discover, context is all. The hoodie as worn by Mark Zuckerberg is the symbol of Silicon Valley culture. The hoodie as worn by young Black men in an urban setting is a perceived threat, one that makes them potentially more likely to be subject to racial profiling and being stopped by the police. Kate Moss is the "epitome of cool" in her trench coat, according to the *Daily Mail*, while Melania Trump was a kind of android First Lady in hers. Stilettos are "sizzling" (the *Daily Mail* again) when worn by a Real Housewife, but it's different when they're worn by trans women in New York. According to organizations including the New York City Bar Association, these women are profiled by police through what they are wearing under the Loitering for the Purpose of Prostitution law, or what has become known as the "walking while trans" law. With marginalized communities particularly at risk, simply a choice of footwear could result in arrest. The objects here may be unremarkable, then, but once on the body – and very much depending on which body – their meaning is varied and nuanced.

I knew early on that what we wear has power, and changes fates. As the child of a mod, details like the precise roundness of a trainer's toe or the specific button-down on a shirt mattered. Like most teenagers, I also learned the hard way how fashions change within the blink of an

Simple, but effective: Sade's masterclass of minimal dressing – jeans and a denim shirt – still has few equals

eye, finally scoring the Dr Martens worn by the cool crowd at school on the week where they had moved on to army boots; or – before the vintage boom hit – worrying endlessly about the judgement of school friends if they found out what I was wearing was secondhand, as opposed to brand-spanking new and from Naf Naf. This love of vintage – which dates back to a V-neck jumper bought at the age of 14 for 20p – perhaps piqued my interest in the stories of clothing. I was intrigued by a disconnect: how the very same item of clothing can, in just in a few years, change its connotations entirely. How, for example, me in 2019 buying an 80s grey-and-black checked dress to wear as a bit of a nod to Balenciaga's recent collections, is probably a very different take from the intentions of the original wearer, when she bought her frock – for the office? – at BHS back in the day.

Working in fashion journalism for 20 years, I have seen trends come and go. I have written about everything from my love of pyjamas (it's real) to the unexpected return of the wellington boot. Reporting on fashion shows, I have seen some amazing, glamorous, out-of-this-world things. Chanel turning the Grand Palais into a double-C branded supermarket. Barry Manilow singing "Copacabana" flanked by supermodels. Extinction Rebellion staging a funeral for fashion at London Fashion Week. A Paris street scene recreated by Louis Vuitton in Paris (meta), with (squeak!) Frank Ocean on the front row, and Héctor Bellerín on the catwalk. For me, though, these moments are only part of the story. I have always been far more fascinated by clothes away from the catwalk, by what people choose to wear every day – to go to work, to dinner, to a nightclub – and how outfits tell others all about who we are.

When it comes to style, the people I admire aren't those posing on red carpets, with their stylists just out of shot. It's the ones who use clothes to say something. See William S Burroughs in his businessman drag, Sade's take-me-as-I-am simplicity, *Grey Gardens'* Little Edie in headscarves and diamante out to shock East Hampton, Prince in

*Forever cool: Chloe Sevigny bringing quirk to the LBD
in 1996 with some tiger-stripe tights. Swoon*

his trench coat and underpants, Chloë Sevigny in tiger-print tights
in 1996, Jarvis Cocker around the same time in cord and nylon,
Zendaya and her sadgirl hoodie in *Euphoria*. I aim to learn from the
example of these luminaries, to make clothes work for me, as they do
for them. I might signal to the like-minded with a B-52s T-shirt, wear
a miniskirt to express that carefree feeling on the first warm day of
the year, or blend in at a party full of strangers by wearing an LBD.

Not everyone appreciates the power of style. A few years ago,
I swapped the usual round of fashion shows in February for a trip

around south-east Asia. In the jungle in Borneo, I got chatting –
inevitably – to the other Brits staying in the same place that I was.
When the – again, inevitable – question arose about what we all
did for a living, I told them I worked as a fashion journalist. The
disapproval and disdain was palpable. "Ooh, *fashion*," responded
one of the group, with a roll of the eyes. What this charming
individual didn't register was that he, just like the rest of us, used his
clothes to both express his personality and, unwittingly, tell others
about himself. Just because he was wearing a Chang beer T-shirt,
climbing shoes and a pair of drawstring shorts didn't mean he
was exempt. In fact, I could easily ascertain that he was a typical
"traveller" signalling his "alternative" view to other travellers, as well
as (inadvertently) the fact that he came from a more conventional
background than he might like to let on. Because our clothes speak
for us even if we don't say a word – and they don't always say what
we want them to.

I'm not the first person to work this out. Roland Barthes,
Dick Hebdige and Walter Benjamin are only three names who
have thought far more deeply than me about fashion, clothes and
semiotics. More recently, novelist Marlon James, when discussing
clothes, said, "putting on external things can get you closer to the
core of who you are", while Henry Holland has talked about his
fascination with clothing as "a form of emotional expression, telling
the world who we are and how we feel". Miuccia Prada calls fashion
an "instant language", and, in her 1981 book, *The Language of Clothes*,
Alison Lurie – at least 30 years before Mrs Prada – clarified that
there isn't a sort of sartorial Esperanto. "Within every language
of clothes there are many different dialects and accents, some
almost unintelligible to members of the mainstream culture," Lurie
writes.[1] How that language shifts over time, place and community
is, ultimately, what interests me. I hope, as you read these stories, it
interests you too – whatever you happen to be wearing today.

THE WHITE T-SHIRT

I have always wanted to be a white T-shirt woman. Jane Birkin, sun-dappled, on a French street in the 70s. Diana Ross with wet hair on the cover of *Diana* in 1980. Jourdan Dunn or any supposedly off-duty model. But I default to letting my clothes start the conversation, speaking to my tastes, likes and world view – so my T-shirt might feature a cartoon character, a Beychella pyramid, Dennis Bergkamp. A plain white T-shirt rises above such blatant semaphores. It's a sartorial humblebrag – one that allows its wearer's uniqueness, their coolness, their charisma, their beauty, to shine through.

It didn't start out that way. The white T-shirt's ancestors weren't seen by many people at all. T-shaped shirts, made of cotton, silk or linen, were worn under clothes by both men and women from the medieval era onwards as a way to keep sweat off more costly outer layers, and promote cleanliness (these garments could be washed more easily).

JULY 13, 1942 **10** CENTS
YEARLY SUBSCRIPTION $4.50

A real American hero: the white T-shirt
joins the war effort in 1942

FROM UNDERWEAR
TO UNIFORM

THEY WERE FAR FROM sexy, but an erotic charge came from
a glimpse of such undershirts, particularly on women, who were
otherwise covered from head to foot. These items were, as costume
historian Lucy Adlington writes, "an inevitable prelude to nudity".[1]

The first T-shirts that we might recognize came courtesy of a
Victorian-era drive to hygiene. Dr Gustav Jäger, a German hygienist,
recommended the wearing of woollen undershirts. While these would
not have had the close fit that we are used to, the knitted fabric meant
a shift from previous shirt-like designs. The doctor's theories inspired
the foundation of the undershirt-making brand Jaeger – originally
called Dr Jaeger's Sanitary Woollen System – by British businessman
Lewis Tomalin in 1880. It joined Sunspel: founded in 1860, they were
producing Sea Island cotton T-shirts by 1877.

Soon-to-be household names were being established in the States.
Fruit of the Loom, the oldest registered trademark in the country, was
founded in 1851, initially selling textiles. Jockey, originally ST Cooper
and Sons, arrived in 1876. And Hanes was founded in 1901. All three
made what was known as the "union suit", a jumpsuit worn under
clothes. At the start of the twentieth century, this item was cut in half
– to become long johns and a sort of T-shirt. The cotton crop that
made the fabric for T-shirts would likely have been grown by poor,
Black sharecroppers in the South, the children or grandchildren of
slaves – these early T-shirts, like many cotton goods, have their place
on the timeline of racial oppression.

Hanes, in 1901, manufactured cotton T-shirts for the US Navy,
and so did Fruit of the Loom in the 1910s.[2] By 1913, they were
officially part of the uniform.[3] The British Royal Navy had similar

items in the late nineteenth century, and sailors sometimes wore them without an outer layer, should they be conducting a particularly physical task. The probably apocryphal story goes that sleeves were first sewn onto the sleeveless woollen undershirts that sailors wore when a navy crew knew Queen Victoria was due to visit a ship, because men's armpits were deemed unseemly. France also had a part to play in the popularization of the T-shirt: American soldiers who were part of the Expeditionary Forces army in the First World War, then wearing long-sleeved wool undershirts, were envious of the more practical cotton designs of their French counterparts because they dried more quickly in the damp environment of the trenches. They brought these designs home.

An alliance between the American man and the white T-shirt was beginning. It was helped by developing ideals of masculinity: the elite athlete, the working man and the soldier. The rise of sports in colleges from the 30s[4] meant the T-shirt was moving beyond underwear, and worn for running and by off-duty athletes (Fruit of the Loom supplied colleges with T-shirts from the 1910s).[5] This college connection was set by 1920 – the first known citation of the word "T-shirt" comes in F Scott Fitzgerald's debut novel, *This Side of Paradise*, where it's listed as an item that protagonist Amory Blaine takes to "New England, the land of schools". At the same time, working men took up the T-shirt as a useful item when carrying out manual labour, whether on a farm or at sea.[6] By 1938, Fruit of the Loom, Hanes, and Sears, Roebuck & Co were mass-producing T-shirts, selling them for 24 cents (around $4.40 in today's money).[7] In 1942, the US Army adopted the T-shirt.[8] It was still officially an undergarment, but it was popular with soldiers – and part of their image. A soldier training in the Air Corps featured on the front of *Life* magazine in 1942. In a tight T-shirt, showing off his biceps and cradling a machine gun, he's the archetypal American hero.

HEROES AND REBELS

BRANDS REALIZED THAT this association was a branding opportunity. "You needn't be a soldier to have your own personal T-shirt," read a Sears, Roebuck & Co catalogue slogan from the 40s.[9] The eroticism of the tight-fit practical item was the undeniable subtext. Michelle Millar Fischer describes brands as "using a strangely ambiguous rhetoric ... focusing on the image of the virile, heteronormative soldier or dad on the one hand, while offering the homoerotic signifier of the taut male torso on the other."[10]

This was only strengthened post-war (a period when a woman in a T-shirt would have been highly unusual). Marlon Brando was the pin-up, with his breakout role as Stanley Kowalski in Tennessee Williams's 1947 play *A Streetcar Named Desire*. Brando's tight white T-shirt signalled he was a working man and ex-soldier, a foil to Blanche DuBois's Southern belle airs and graces. It also serves another purpose – clinging to every muscle, the T-shirt reveals to DuBois a sexiness that couldn't be tamed by the civilizing suit.

When Brando reprised Kowalski in the film in 1951, his smouldering presence made him a sex symbol overnight. It also put the T-shirt on the radar of an emerging generation. Brando in *The Wild One* two years later – in a white T-shirt he was reportedly sewn into – continued on a theme, as did a young Elvis, and James Dean in *Rebel Without a Cause* in 1955, in jeans, blouson jacket and white T-shirt.[11] The few actors of colour in cinema at that time were portrayed wearing white T-shirts too. Sidney Poitier, playing a juvenile delinquent in 1955's *Blackboard Jungle*, wore one. So did Harry Belafonte, as a politician in an interracial relationship in 1957's *Island in the Sun*. All of this made it seem like an item of danger, even an item of change. The conservative establishment became anti-T-shirt – they were frequently banned at schools.[12] Patriotism had been the catalyst

*An item of rebellion: Sidney Poitier as the mid-century
juvenile delinquent, in the white T-shirt*

to bring the white T-shirt to the civilian wardrobe in a bid to emulate soldier heroes. Young people were even keener to emulate their rebel heroes. With this factor, the white T-shirt changed from undergarment to uniform to bona fide fashion item.

The T-shirt as sandwich board was arriving. In 1948, Republican presidential candidate Thomas Dewey supposedly distributed T-shirts with "Dew-it-with-Dewey" during his campaign (if the story is true, few took him up on the offer; Truman won a second term).[13] By the 1950s, children's T-shirts featured everyone from Davy Crockett to Mickey Mouse. The rock T-shirt wasn't far behind – it's believed the first was an Elvis design from 1956, apparently produced by his manager Colonel Tom Parker.[14] As screen-printing became easier from the late 50s, this corner of the T-shirt market flourished. T-shirts even had a part in Beatlemania – it was possible to buy Beatles T-shirts during their first tour of the States in 1964.[15] By the mid-60s, they were worn on anti-Vietnam protests, with slogans like "Make love, not war".[16]

With the 60s came perhaps the first notable fashion moment for a woman in a T-shirt: Jean Seberg in *À Bout de Souffle*, the Jean-Luc Godard film, in 1960. Playing a young American in Paris, selling the *New York Herald Tribune*, she wears a T-shirt with the newspaper's logo on it and pair of cropped black trousers. Seberg was the embodiment of a new take on beauty: the gamine. As Dennita Sewell writes, the T-shirt was essential to this, because it "showed off her curvaceous figure and at the same time embodied a new, youthful androgynous style of seduction and feminine power".[17] Luxury labels soon saw something here – brands like Pierre Balmain and Christian Dior sold silk T-shirts in the 60s, in line with a shift towards more casual dress codes and these different ideas of elegance.

By this point, the eroticism of the man in the white T-shirt had given the item a place in the style pantheon of gay culture. It was part of a look for a generation who in 1967, in the UK, finally saw gay sex partially decriminalized. Playwright Joe Orton was a poster boy, wearing a bright white T-shirt, cuffed jeans and sneakers. "He refused to fit into the 1960s stereotype of a fey gay man," writes Terry Newman in *Legendary Authors and the Clothes They Wore*. "In the theatrical world, his informal sartorial signature set him apart from the typical booted and suited brigade."[18]

Sex, shock and slogans

ORTON'S PLACE IN the history of the T-shirt continued after his early death. Punk pioneers Vivienne Westwood and Malcolm McLaren named their shop Sex in 1974, after reading an entry in Orton's diary which read: "Sex is the only way to infuriate them."[19] The T-shirts for sale in store were both powerful social commentary and, sometimes, highly offensive. One of these depicted a gay orgy, combined with the title of Orton's biography, *Prick Up Your Ears*. Others included Disney characters having sex, the now-famous trouserless cowboys with their penises touching, an image of breasts where the wearer's breasts would be, swastikas, chicken bones and sex offenders. "The perverse and the abnormal were valued intrinsically," wrote Dick Hebdige of punk.[20] Adjacent to punk was the skinhead scene, where the white T-shirt was worn with tight jeans, braces and Dr Martens as part of a look that celebrated working-class heroes. While initially multicultural, it's a scene now associated with the National Front. In this context, the white T-shirt is the uniform of the racist.

The 70s also saw the emergence of the white T-shirt woman. Jane Birkin made it part of that South of France look, Joan Didion smoked in one and Patti Smith wore one printed with a photo of a grinning Keith Richards. A T-shirt ad's slogan called it "the piece of clothing that emancipated America's top half".[21] On these women, the T-shirt spoke to an effortless female confidence – although, notably, not everyone was allowed to opt out of effort. White T-shirt women in the 70s were all white, middle class and thin.

*A white T-shirt woman: Jane Birkin's effortless chic, with
white T-shirt, jeans and French sunshine in 1974*

Printing with customized messages was commonplace. Sewell
says that department store Gimbels (of *Elf* fame) claimed to sell 1,000
of these T-shirts per week in 1976, and the "I Love NY" T-shirt was
created in 1977.[22] Designed by Milton Glaser, it was commissioned
by the New York State Department when the city had a billion-dollar
deficit and massive unemployment.[23] The T-shirt, worn by New Yorkers
and visitors alike, was an instant hit, speaking of solidarity and hope.

A much-cited T-shirt moment dates to 1975, and Labyris Books,
the first women's bookshop in New York. They made a T-shirt that
reads "The Future Is Female", and photographer Liza Cowan took
a picture of her then-partner, musician Alix Dobkin, wearing it.

*An original: the 1975 T-shirt that, 40 years and
the invention of Instagram later, spawned
a thousand imitators*

Designer Rachel Berks spotted the image on the @h_e_r_s_t_o_r_y Instagram account in 2015 and recreated the T-shirt. It became a favourite of modern feminists, including St Vincent, Cara Delevingne and – when it was swiftly copied – anyone else shopping on Etsy. There was a luxury version in 2016: Maria Grazia Chiuri, the first female Creative Director at Dior, included a T-shirt with the title of Chimamanda Ngozi Adichie's book *We Should All Be Feminists* in her first collection for the brand.

The white T-shirt was involved in parts of 70s culture that were problematic, too – see the wet T-shirt contest. The *Cultural Encyclopedia of the Breast* dates the phenomenon to a scene in 1977's *The Deep*, where Jacqueline Bisset swims underwater in a thin white T-shirt. But the *Palm Beach Post* in 1975 has the first known example of the term, with a headline "Wet T-shirt Contests Pack Pubs". Reporting on college girls baring their breasts for $75 prize money during spring break, the writer comments: "It may be enough to make feminists choke on their NOW buttons." By the end of the 70s, depending on the context – and the person wearing it – the T-shirt could spell rebellion, racism, sex appeal, objectification, protest or punk.

An item for everyone

THE FOLLOWING DECADE, the T-shirt was worn by all sorts of people, for all sorts of reasons. The white T-shirt had star power again in the 80s due to its connection to iconic rebels like Brando, Dean and Poitier. Like 30 years before, it was often teamed with its sartorial best friend, the blue jean. The combination was worn by Ferris Bueller on his day off in 1986, by dreamboat Morten Harket in the animated video for A-ha's "Take on Me" in 1985, by all three of Bananarama and by Diana Ross.

The printed T-shirt was big business – the *New Yorker* reported that the industry sold 32 million dozen items in 1982.[24] Creatives realized this allowed them to get messages – and their work – out there. Keith Haring, the artist who started by completing drawings on subway platforms, opened Pop Shop in 1986 as a way to bring his art beyond the gallery. T-shirts with his trademark babies, TVs and more were a major part of that, and ahead of their time. Thanks to things like Pop Shop, a wearable allegiance to a certain artist is now as possible as it is for a favourite band. Haring, meanwhile, has gone mega-mass – his work is found on T-shirts at Uniqlo for £12.90 a go.

Haring also used the T-shirt as a way to speak out against a new threat: AIDS. Silence=Death became a popular slogan in the gay community after community group Act Up began using it on posters from 1987, and Haring transferred this to T-shirts, adding his cartoon-like figures. At the same time, the T-shirt was a way for the American Black middle classes to assert themselves. Author and film-maker Nelson George writes that this was the year T-shirts with slogans like "It's a Black Thing. You Wouldn't Understand" became popular at colleges that had a predominantly Black student population.

Arguably the biggest T-shirt moment in the 80s, however, was in Downing Street. Katharine Hamnett was invited to Prime Minister Margaret Thatcher's reception after winning Designer of the Year in 1984. Hamnett, a consistently political designer, recognized a photo opportunity. She wore a T-shirt that read "58% DON'T WANT PERSHING", a reference to the American nuclear missiles found across Europe, to meet Thatcher. "I opened my jacket so the writing would be completely legible to the photographers in the room," Hamnett told *The Guardian*. "She [Thatcher] looked down and said, 'You seem to be wearing a rather strong message on your T-shirt' … [she] let out a squawk, like a chicken." Hamnett's message was spread. She was on *News at Ten*, and her T-shirt was spotted on *Top of the Pops* and in fashion magazines.[25] The style was then endlessly imitated – by

Wham! and Frankie Goes to Hollywood at the time, and designer Henry Holland more recently.

The T-shirt was a staple of youth culture in the 80s. It came branded and box-fresh in hip-hop, as groups like Public Enemy, Beastie Boys and NWA testified. In 1988's so-called Second Summer of Love, the smiley face covered ravers' T-shirts across the UK. Coming to the scene on the logo of Danny Rampling's seminal club Shoom, the smiley quickly "swept the country as the logo of acid fashion," Jon Savage wrote in *The Guardian*. But such a happy symbol was quickly vilified when the unease about another generation of young people in T-shirts began: "As acid house became acieed that year, the Smiley flip-flopped from dream symbol to harbinger of wickedness."

Of course, when something is vilified, it becomes fodder for counterculture. The smiley face was reimagined by Nirvana in 1992, when a T-shirt – black this time – hit their merch stands, with a squiggly smile, and two Xs for eyes (it remains popular with alienated teenagers nearly 30 years later). The same year, Cobain wore a Daniel Johnston T-shirt to the MTV Video Music Awards. Johnston, then an obscure name, was signed by Atlantic Records as a result.[26]

The T-shirt as resistance banner came in the form of Malcolm X T-shirts. With slogans like "Our own black shining Prince", a quote from a eulogy at X's funeral, they were worn by a newly politicized generation of young Black people. Part of what the *LA Times* called "Malcolmania", prompted by Spike Lee's 1992 biopic, these T-shirts so upset the establishment that some wearers were – once again – sent home from school.[27]

The white T-shirt was a defining element of the style of Cholo, the Mexican-American subculture. Here it was oversized, and teamed with plaid shirts, baggy jeans, boots and tattoos, as part of a look influenced by what migrant workers wore, and what was worn in prisons. The T-shirt featured painstakingly ironed creases, as if straight out of the box. The fit was part of standing out from all-American

By any means necessary: young people in T-shirts
promoting Spike Lee's 1992 Malcolm X

norms. Speaking to the website *Love Aesthetics*, a self-identified Cholo known only as Chris says, "The baggier the clothes you wore, the more you showed that you were rebellious towards what society expected from you." This sort of resistance appealed across other disenfranchised youth: Cholo style, including that crisp XL white tee, influenced wider African-American street culture, and the look has spread to Japan and Thailand.

The white T-shirt in cinema of the early 90s was about subverting what was now an icon of Americana. Louise wears one, accessorized with a revolver and a 50s convertible, in *Thelma & Louise*. And a young Johnny Depp, stylized as 50s dreamboat Cry-Baby Walker in John Waters's 1990 movie *Cry-Baby*, wears a white T-shirt, biker jacket and quiff. An outfit like this signposts what the trailer spells out – Walker is "born to be bad".

The T-shirt as fashion statement was beginning in the 1990s too. Designers like Giorgio Armani and Helmut Lang wore T-shirts, and labels likes James Perse began to make expensive plain T-shirts a status item. Skate and surf brands including Bape, Stüssy and FUCT provided an alternative take, with logos front and centre, and a if-you-know-you-know kind of feel. This was cemented in 1994 with the arrival of Supreme.[28] The brand, that provokes actual riots with its limited "drops", began with three T-shirts, one with their now-classic box logo. While Supreme T-shirts are not exclusive because of pricing – they cost around £49, nothing compared to, say, a £980 Gucci number – scarcity adds to the cultural currency. They are also about actual currency: the resale market means Supreme T-shirts cost £49, but end up selling for thousands.

TALL TEES AND HIPSTER T-SHIRTS

BY THE TURN of the millennium, the white T-shirt was used by different communities to communicate different things. The so-called "Tall Tee", a long and wide white T-shirt, shows how an item can transition between demographics.

Galaxy, the brand that are known for producing these T-shirts – which go up to 8XL – were worn by young American women at college in the 80s, who wanted a big T-shirt that doubled as a nightdress, a so-called "dorm-tee". Twenty years later, this had fallen out of fashion, but the Tall Tee had a new fanbase – typically young men of colour in urban centres, who picked up these T-shirts sometimes five at a time for $25, potentially throwing away each one after wearing it to ensure the bright white colour each time.

The people who were buying these T-shirts meant they were used as a means of profiling, and banned in schools for fear the item was implicated in gang culture. In 2004, they featured in a storyline in Baltimore-set crime series *The Wire*. Bubbles, a long-time character with drug abuse issues, supplements his income by selling what he calls "whiteys" from his shopping trolley. In 2005, Gadi Dechter wrote an article in the *Baltimore City Paper* about the Tall Tee, garnering opinions on the trend. Music journalist Peter Shapiro says it's about style: "There's the idea of not only living large, but living extra-large, and wearing a long shirt that goes down to your knees is a bold statement." Others link it to a kind of camouflage. "If the cops are looking for a suspect, [he's invariably wearing a] long white T-shirt with long shorts," comments Stuart Silberman from Baltimore store Changes. "So they can't be identified."

Whatever the motivation, this under-the-radar item had already gone beyond its urban habitat. In 2000, Eminem performed at the MTV Video Music Awards in a Tall Tee surrounded by an army of identikit young men in the same outfit. Sean "Puffy" Combs also wore one, as did Jay-Z and Lil Jon. But its sheer popularity and affordability ensured the Tall Tee was a leveller between celebrities and fans. One estimate put the number of Galaxy Tall Tees sold in a year close to three million.

A brand catering to another demographic – soon to be lazily known as "hipsters" – was also doing pretty well with T-shirts at this point. American Apparel, founded by Dov Charney, began producing their own clothes in 2003, with the aim of providing basics for those with a design sensibility that approved of a Helvetica logo. Its sales soared, with an apparent 525 per cent growth by 2005. Part of this was through T-shirts. By 2009, the 2001 fine jersey shirt was a bestseller.[29] Ostensibly plain, the skinny fit inspired by the 70s became a subtle sign of cool in cities ranging from Berlin to Montreal and London, where billboards featured Terry Richardson's questionable ad campaigns of young women wearing these T-shirts with short shorts and knee socks. It all collapsed as Charney's and Richardson's history of alleged sexual harassment was uncovered in 2014. Suddenly those adverts looked much darker, and no one wanted Helvetica on their labels anymore.

NEW, OLD, WHITE – AND MORE

WHILE AMERICAN APPAREL has relaunched, it's fair to say its moment has passed. But the white T-shirt is still indisputably cool. It's the kind of item where the search for the perfect version is seen as a noble and worthwhile pursuit. The Row – the Olsen twins' fashion line, which began in 2006 – started with a mission to create the ultimate T-shirt. Whether or not they have achieved it is debatable, but a Row T-shirt could now be yours for £300.

The anonymity of the white T-shirt cemented its place as a mainstay of normcore style. Working in opposition to the idea of fashionable people as brightly coloured peacocks, this look instead wilfully fetishized the plain: supermarket jeans, grey marl sweatshirts, chunky trainers, white T-shirts. In 2014, *The Cut* deemed it "Fashion for Those Who Realize They're One in 7 Billion".

Anonymity is not to everyone's taste: as a blank canvas, the white T-shirt is also in the arsenal of activism. This runs from "No justice, no peace" T-shirts seen on Black Lives Matter protesters, to the T-shirt as an Instagram-friendly sandwich board to broadcast thoughts on almost every matter. Since Berks's "The Future Is Female" T-shirt, the feminist message has sadly been so commodified as to be almost meaningless, but other messages cut through. Memorable examples include the Corbynite Nike swoosh T-shirt of 2017, "Frankie Says Fuck Brexit", Martine Rose's arch "Promising Britain" design, Balenciaga's 2017 Bernie Sanders tribute and "Fuck Boris", a statement seen as so provocative that its wearer was almost arrested in 2020. A message that everyone can get behind comes in the form of the NHS T-shirt – Sports Banger's bootleg design pairing the health service's logo and that of a Nike swoosh – first made in 2015. It became particularly on point at the height of the pandemic in 2020. Sports Banger sold the T-shirts over three nights in May and made £100,000 for the NHS. While founder Jonny Banger, as he is known, is adamant that activism needs to be more than a T-shirt, it's perhaps a good place to start.

For the majority of people, T-shirts are still basics. As such, they can be shockingly cheap. A pack of three is available at Sainsbury's for £3. That's the same price as a meal deal. No wonder the T-shirt is at the centre of the environmental debate. Around two billion were purchased in 2012, and they're discarded pretty quickly.[30] UN data shows the equivalent of 276 million secondhand T-shirts were shipped to Mozambique in 2017.[31] The production has its impact too – up to 11,000 litres of water are used for every kilogram of cotton grown, and the cotton industry accounts for 24 per cent of all pesticide use, affecting growers' health and that of the environment.[32] Think about that the next time you chuck a pack of three white tees in the shopping trolley. Organic cotton T-shirts are better – using 186 gallons of water compared to 2,168 for non-organic. Arket, Cos, Colorful Standard and Weekday are brands to look at.

Or maybe new T-shirts aren't necessary at all. The old ones already to be found in your wardrobe can often be more appealing – the pieces that genuinely spark joy, the one you put on when you have had a bad day. In Emily Spivack's lovely book *Worn in New York*, about writers' and celebrities' favoured items, T-shirts come up frequently in stories told by people ranging from Adam Horovitz to Eileen Myles. "Even though it's ragged, it's a piece of authenticating clothing," writes Myles of a grey, faded, holey T-shirt. "I wear it and feel like the world is in place."[33] I might not be a white T-shirt woman, but this is a concept I can get behind. I have a brick-yellow T-shirt that belonged to my mum in the 80s – it's so tattered that a friend once said I looked "shipwrecked" when I was wearing it. But I'll always treasure it. Just as Myles says, when I wear it I feel like the world is in place.

A wearable placard: Martine Rose's comment on Brexit makes its way down the catwalk in 2019

HOW TO WEAR
THE WHITE T-SHIRT NOW

Find your fit
Your perfect white T-shirt is a personal thing. Wear yours skintight or oversized, cropped or long. This is the kind of item where you can set your preferences, and change depending on mood. Brands with cult followings include Cos, APC and Sunspel.

Wear with jeans for a stone-cold classic outfit
There's a reason we have worn this outfit for 70 years – jeans and T-shirts go together like burgers and fries. The combination is a no-brainer, as seen on Jourdan Dunn or James Dean. Go with dark indigo denim for the full effect – it makes the white pop.

Alternatively, mix it up
The white T-shirt lends itself well to the kind of outfit where the action is on the lower half. Think of it as a quiet foil to your PVC skirt, 90s-style shorts or trousers covered in cats. For example.

Utilize the slogan T-shirt
The T-shirt has a new role – it's a way to tell passers-by what you believe in, to – as Katharine Hamnett did – get the message out there (note: this works even if you're not meeting the prime minister).

Look after it
No one wants an off-white T-shirt. To keep whites white without resorting to planet-zapping chemicals, Martha Stewart recommends adding lemon juice to your wash. Thanks for the tip, Martha.

NEED TO KNOW

- Before there were T-shirts, there were T-shaped shirts, worn as underwear. The garment we recognize came about at the start of the twentieth century. It was soon part of the kit of the navy in Britain, France and the US, and also worn by athletes and working men.

- Post-war, the white T-shirt became the symbol of the bad boy – spurred on by cinematic examples like Marlon Brando, James Dean and Sidney Poitier. All of this made it seem like an item of danger, perhaps even an item of change. The T-shirt was banned in some schools.

- Words on T-shirts date back to 1948 and a campaign for presidential candidate Thomas Dewey. They have since shocked with punk, protested during Vietnam and got arty with Keith Haring. The first T-shirt "moment" for women featured words – when Jean Seberg wore a T-shirt with "New York Herald Tribune" on it in 1960's *À Bout de Souffle*.

- White T-shirts have been worn oversized by those outside of mainstream society – including Mexican-American Cholos, and young people of colour who adopted the 8XL Tall Tee in the 00s. Perhaps the sheer size of these meant they were seen as threatening – the establishment linked them to gang culture.

- As a blank canvas, the white T-shirt is now in the arsenal of activism. See the "No justice, no peace" T-shirts seen on Black Lives Matter protesters and Sports Banger's NHS/Nike bootleg T-shirt. Sold during 2020's coronavirus pandemic, it raised £100,000 for the NHS.

Martine Rose
Fashion designer

When Martine Rose was designing her logo T-shirt in 2014, there was a problem she didn't foresee: namely, it would be hard for Martine Rose to wear a Martine Rose T-shirt. "What really put me off, the nail in the coffin, was going to all of these coffee shops where they ask for your name," she says, breaking out into a grin. "Honestly, every time I wore the bloody T-shirt I had to say my name for some reason."

Of course, people who aren't called Martine Rose can wear the T-shirt untroubled, and many do: it's a bestseller for the London brand. While Martine Rose the label sells everything from shirts to suits, made for men but also worn by women, the T-shirt remains central to its identity. "[The T-shirt is] completely democratic, you can really pull people in," says Rose, as two design assistants pin some images to a moodboard that is leaning up against the studio wall behind her desk. "You can create this sort of weird and wonderful collection and somehow anchor the story in the T-shirts."

Rose, who was born into a Jamaican-British family in south London in 1980, began her menswear label in 2007. It has a unique point of view that takes in youth culture and the current zeitgeist, but also re-evaluates the mundane in an offbeat – often appreciative – way. Her clothes have been inspired by bus conductors and bike messengers, and her shows have been hosted in venues including a Tottenham market and her daughter's school. Rose regularly draws upon her adolescence and life journey – in particular, her family and friends growing up in the late 80s and early 90s. This is relevant for her love of T-shirts. "Apart from my children, if my house was on fire I would grab my acid smiley T-shirt that I have had since I was nine," she says. "My cousin was really into raves so in 1989, he gave me this BOY London T-shirt … it takes me back to all of these really important moments around that time, watching my cousin go out and be a part of this thing, and knowing that there was this other world that I couldn't access yet but couldn't wait – I literally couldn't wait."

Arguably, formative experiences like this shaped the kind of designer that Rose grew up to be. She says, "If anyone had one of my T-shirts in 30 years, it [would be] like the biggest honour", so she knows the power of these humble items. She has also used T-shirts to make statements – such as in 2019, when a Brexit message was part of a collection, and Rose made a T-shirt featuring a clown dressed as a politician. "We were just bombarded with these jokers all day every day talking shit about Brexit," she remembers. "I mean it was everywhere; it was impossible to not comment on it."

As well as including T-shirts in her collections, Rose – as the smiley anecdote testifies – wears T-shirts herself, and does so almost every day. She said she has a collection of hundreds, including vintage, Hanes white classics, and ones by skate brands including Aries and Supreme. Today, she is wearing a vintage white T-shirt featuring a map of Africa coloured red, gold and green, and the slogan "Free South Africa". "Clothes are interesting because they are the most intimate thing in that we wear them closest to our skin," she says. "When you see someone wearing a powerful T-shirt or a T-shirt that says something, you understand that the person wearing it really believes in that message." For Rose, a T-shirt can express anything from anti-racism to a devotion to rave or the dislike of Brexit. But wearing your own name? That might be a step too far.

THE MINISKIRT

"The home of the gnome and the ordinary citizen." That's how poet and writer John Betjeman described Neasden in 1973. He clearly wasn't aware of an exception to his rule for the area in north-west London: Lesley Hornby, born and raised in Neasden. You might know her as Twiggy.

Before she was Twiggy, 16-year-old Lesley *was* pretty ordinary – she went to school and worked as a Saturday girl at the local hairdresser. Then, in 1965, Lesley started dating Nigel Davies – or, as he liked to be called, Justin de Villeneuve. A friend of De Villeneuve's thought Lesley – a 5'6" six-and-a-half stone slip of a thing with a penchant for extreme eyelashes – might make a potential model. De Villeneuve, seizing the opportunity, transported her far away from Neasden – to the smart Mayfair hair salon, Leonard's. Here, she gained a new haircut, a new name – Twiggy – and a new set of beauty shots taken by rising photography star Barry Lategan.

*Worthy of the nickname: with twiglike legs,
Lesley Hornby – aka Twiggy – was the poster
girl for the miniskirt*

Mary, Lesley
and Barbara

AFTER DABBLING IN modelling for a few months, Twiggy got her big break early in 1966, when the *Daily Express*'s fashion editor spotted her photographs at Leonard's. On 23 February, the teenager appeared in the newspaper with the headline, "I NAME THIS GIRL THE FACE OF '66".[1] Twiggy wore bell-bottom cords and a skinny-rib jumper in those images. But she quickly became the poster girl of that most 60s of items: the miniskirt. If her twig-like legs earned her that new moniker, they were now her USP – they gave her a look of knock-kneed innocence perfect for a moment where youth was the newest currency. American *Vogue* declared her "the mini-girl in the mini-era".

By 1966, the miniskirt – named after that other 60s design classic, the Mini Cooper car – was already worn by young women around the world. But the first fashion designer to raise hemlines so dramatically is a matter of debate. André Courrèges, the French designer known for his futuristic aesthetic and use of synthetic fabrics, put short A-line skirts on the catwalk in 1964 as part of his *Space Age* collection. Marit Allen – the influential editor of British *Vogue*'s "Young Idea" section – was adamant that London designer John Bates was the first to do minis. In truth, the design had been in development for a while. The V&A points to Cristóbal Balenciaga's 1957 sack dress, which sat on the knee, and Yves Saint Laurent's 1959 trapeze design for Christian Dior, which hit just above it, as nascent examples.

Even before this, though, the mini existed – on the streets and in imaginations. It had been a regular in costumes for sci-fi films and comics since the late 1940s. And then there were schoolgirls. The St Trinian's films began in the mid-50s – with 1954's *The Belles of St Trinian's* the UK's third most popular film of the year. In it, the sixth form girls are played as "sexpots" in short skirts, but this fantasy was partly based on a reality we're still familiar with today – that of teenage girls hitching up their school skirts to show off their legs. Twiggy, this time, was no exception. "I always got in trouble for rolling [my skirt] up at the waist to make it shorter," she said in 2019.

Notably, Mary Quant did the same. If Twiggy was the model of the miniskirt, and Courrèges or Bates did it first, the almost-always-miniskirted, much-photographed Quant, with her Vidal Sassoon bob, was instrumental in making it go mass. Writing in her 1965 autobiography *Quant by Quant*, the designer explains how she first began experimenting with the length of her skirt at school "to be more exciting-looking", customizing the uniform and making "the sort of dresses I liked … terribly short and chic".[2] In 1960, when most women would still have been wearing the midi designs of the previous decade, a 26-year-old Quant was photographed in a skirt that exposed her knees. By the mid-60s, her endorsement of the mini was total. She even wore a mini to receive her OBE in 1966.

The designer had been someone to note since the mid-50s. In 1955, with her husband Alexander Plunket Greene, Quant had opened Bazaar, a boutique on the King's Road, fashioned as "a bouillabaisse of clothes and accessories".[3] Initially selling designs made by adapting mail-order patterns, the shop stocked bright, graphic and comfortable clothing and gained so many fans that crowds formed outside the doors. A fashion writer at the time described the scene thus: "Suddenly someone invented a style of dressing which we realized we had been wanting for ages … It gave anyone wearing them a sense of identity with youth and adventure and brightness."[4] Quant, meanwhile, wrote that "The young were tired of wearing essentially the same as their mothers."

While Quant's designs were relatively expensive – a jacket and skirt in 1962 would have been 32 guineas, or around £175 today – younger women or those with less cash to spend could head to Biba.

In his book about Britain in the 60s, *White Heat*, Dominic Sandbrook describes the store as "a shrine to the spending power of youth".[5] Opened by Barbara Hulanicki and her husband Stephen Fitz-Simon in 1963, the couple's venture coincided with the boom in mass-produced clothes; they were able to adopt what the V&A called a "pile it high, sell it cheap" approach – with prices designed to fall within "the maximum disposable weekly income of the average London secretary". And so, the mini became an option for all.

Quant, Hulanicki and Twiggy are crucial to the story of the mini, but they are also familiar characters in a wider story – that of the swinging 60s in London. Now such a cliché that a Google image search is as likely to bring up Austin Powers's "Groovy baby" as it is any archive images, this moment remains seismic in the history of youth culture.

While a large part of British society was still in thrall to the establishment in the 60s – 320,000 people lined the streets for Winston Churchill's funeral in 1965, with 25 million watching on television – certain corners of London, including Carnaby Street and the King's Road, were swinging and in the media spotlight. Here, a different demographic called the shots for the first time. "Youth, once something to endure, transformed in the span of a few years of British sensations into a valuable form of currency," wrote Shawn Levy in his history of swinging London, *Ready, Steady, Go!* "[It was] the font of taste and fashion, the only age, seemingly, that mattered."[6]

The mini symbolized the new, independent, sexually emancipated young women emerging in the decade, emboldened by a new role in the workforce, disposable income, the postwar economic boom, and the impact of the pill, with its rhetoric of sexual freedom. The design, because it exposed women's legs, was undoubtedly in some ways about sexual attraction. But, to those wearing it, the mini was principally about something else – it spelled independence. As Courrèges said, this was a design for "girls who go shopping, run for buses".[7]

Barbara Hulanicki
Fashion designer & founder of Biba

The mechanics of video calls – crackly Wi-Fi connections, delays, battery charge, robot voices and glitchy screens – are the kind of thing that get old quickly. But some people manage to shine through the failures of technology – and Barbara Hulanicki is one of them.

The 84-year-old founder of Biba is a tonic beaming out of my cracked iPhone screen on a grey London afternoon. Hulanicki has been living in Miami for the past 12 years, but, dressed all in black, with her white bob and chunky-framed black glasses, she still has the spirit of 60s London – albeit combined with an impressive tan.

Hulanicki was born in Poland and moved to the UK as a 12-year-old. After studying at art college, she became a fashion illustrator, later setting up as a designer through mail order, working with her husband Stephen Fitz-Simon – whom she called simply Fitz. This is how she first came to prominence – when a design for an on-the-knee gingham dress was featured in the *Daily Mail* in 1964. "We used to go and collect the mail [orders] in Oxford Street," she says. "I was sitting in the car waiting, and Fitz comes around the corner with a sack, saying, 'Wait, there's two more!'"

The couple set up Biba the same year. It was two years later, in 1966, that they had their first proper miniskirt moment. "Our production was right on the nose," she remembers. "We had to get some skirts done in jersey and they had to be dried overnight. When I saw them, my heart sank, they were shrinking. I was in tears, it was such a big order. But then, we put them on the shop floor and they went running out." The designer says it was always the young women shopping in Biba who made the trends happen. Then, as now, they could smell artifice a mile off.

Cathy McGowan – the presenter of *Ready Steady Go!*, the Friday-night music show – was a regular Biba customer, and a kind of Alexa Chung of her day. But even without celebrities, Biba – thanks to a new winning formula of low prices and fashionable items – quickly became quite the scene. This was even despite its unusual location in Kensington, far away from, to use the decade's lingo, where the action was. "We were nothing to do with Carnaby Street. We were quite snobby about that. I can't believe we were in Abingdon Road," says Hulanicki now, genuinely mystified. "But the shop was packed. It was a destination. You have no idea what the Saturdays were like. The boys would come in to meet the girls."

The "girls" were young working women, who wanted a new wardrobe. Does Hulanicki think the miniskirt signalled a new era of women's lib? "Absolutely. It was against the parents, you see. Girls left home and came to London and took bedsits. They had jobs, they were all typing." Biba's success came from providing the whole look: a boot that worked with miniskirts sold out, for example, with queues outside the shop on delivery days. "Legs were sexy in those days, not these awful bosoms. Now it's like a comic strip."

Hulanicki's video has dropped out, so I just see an icon of a younger her, plus the Biba logo, on her screen. With technology no longer on our side, it feels like time to go. But she's just getting started. Hulanicki moves from a story of working on jeans at Fiorucci, to her time living in Brazil, and her thoughts on what young people wear now, compared to then. Much like the miniskirt, in fact, Hulanicki has staying power, and retains the energy of a decade that changed the world.

Whatever the thinking behind it, the sexiness of the mini meant it caused tensions between generations. It went against the existing male ideals of what female virtue looked like – a pretty and passive homemaker in a calf-length frock. Young women were, instead, choosing to wear something that showed their body, owning their own sexuality. They were – or this was the reading – inviting male attention. All that female flesh on display walking down the street, or in offices, distracted respectable men from being respectable.

In 1965, Jean Shrimpton's appearance at the Melbourne Cup wearing a miniskirt five inches about the knee – chaste by modern standards – put her under fire in the media. "Fashion-conscious Derby Day racegoers were horrified," reported Melbourne's *Sun* newspaper. "Insulting", "a disgrace" and "how dare she?" were some of the responses.[8] This trickled down to more ordinary encounters too. Helen Baxter, recalling her adolescence in mod oral history *Ready Steady Girls*, said, "I remember I brought one girl home after art school and she wore a shorter skirt than most dared to wear at that time. My father told me never to bring her back again."[9]

Such disapproval was in vain, however. Thanks in part to mass production, fashion moved at accelerated speed in the 60s, and mini fever took hold. By 1966's Melbourne Cup, Australian newspaper *The Age* wrote of the same event: "Miss Shrimpton would have passed unnoticed in the crowd ... Anyone with hemlines below the knee looked very 'old hat'." The same year, a group of miniskirted young women picketed the Christian Dior atelier in Paris, seemingly irate at the lack of miniskirts in designer Marc Bohan's collections. "Miniskirts forever," read one placard.

Respectability was out, then, and freedom was in. In December 1967, *Time* magazine put the mini on its cover – a symbol of the new laissez-faire demographic. "Ebullient and supremely self-confident," the magazine wrote "the new young style-setters couldn't care less about looking like ladies." Quant saw it as a wearable representation

*A cause worth fighting for: protesters storm Christian
Dior in 1966 in defence of the miniskirt*

of a decade: "The 60s mini was the most self-indulgent, optimistic, 'look at me, isn't life wonderful' fashion ever devised," she said in 2012. "It expressed the 60s, the emancipation of women, the pill and rock'n'roll ... It was the beginning of women's lib."

Indeed, in spite of – or perhaps because of – its role attracting male attention, the miniskirt was embraced by the feminist movement, as a sort of sartorial gauntlet. A brilliant photograph of New York Radical Women group planning their protest of Miss World 1968 features eight miniskirts out of a total of 12 members. The significance of wearing an item of clothing where a woman was able to stride would not have been lost on them – nor would the disruption that the sight of women's legs brought to existing protocols. As costume historian James Laver wrote in 1969, "Short skirts were a symbol of women's emancipation: they meant that women had shaken off their shackles and were 'stepping out'."[10]

The mini as freedom flag: feminists at a 1968 meeting of the New York Radical Women

Flappers and philosophers

THE MINISKIRT WILL FOREVER be associated with the 60s, but it dates further back – even beyond those 40s sci-fi comics. Neolithic sculptures from Serbia show female figures in short skirts, while versions of miniskirts were worn by certain groups in ancient Egypt. But in recent Western history, the 60s style has its most direct precedents in that other decade when youth ran wild: the 20s.

The hemline index – a theory by economist George Taylor – floats the idea that with a more robust economy, women wear shorter skirts. While this has been disputed somewhat in recent years, it holds true for the eras in question here. As with the 60s, the raising of hemlines in the 20s was in line with a growing economy – in the US, it expanded by 42 per cent from 1920. Accordingly, over the decade, the acceptable skirt length went from just above the ankle to just below the knee. Thigh exposure at this point was still only permitted at the beach, or by dancers like Josephine Baker.

Shorter skirts had started to appear during the First World War – ostensibly to pay lip service to rationed fabric, but also to push fashion forward a step. The first shorter silhouette suggested by Paris designers (still the ones that the rest of the world looked to at this point) was the so-called "war crinoline" from around 1915, which exposed the wearer's ankles.[11] The "barrel", from around 1917, was narrower, reflecting the leaner times of three years of war, and shorter.[12]

Although fabric shortage was a factor initially, short skirts stayed in fashion after the war – and indeed got shorter. A depleted generation of young people – sometimes called the Lost Generation, due to how many casualties they endured – wanted to have fun.

Enter, depending on where you were living, the jazzer, the flapper or the Bright Young Thing. Zelda Fitzgerald – wife of F Scott and quintessential flapper – summed up the mood; one of living moment to moment. In her autobiographical story *Eulogy on the Flapper*, she wrote that "She was conscious that the things she did were the things she had always wanted to do." Across the pond, columnist Patrick Balfour referred to the Bright Young Things as "a community of impulse". The shorter skirts, worn with the newly fashionable bob, were expressions of a new spontaneity. And both were much more conducive to doing the Charleston.

The young women wearing these items were the children of Victorians – a culture so prudish that table legs were covered up because they too closely resembled the real thing. The shorter skirt became a scandalous example of the moral looseness of young women – and the breakdown in society such behaviour entailed. Some states in the US tried to ban "skirts higher than three inches above the ankle", while a journalist writing in *The Times* in 1920 warned against extending the vote to women under 30, saying the "scantily clad, jazzing flapper [sees] a dance, a new hat or a man with a car is of more importance than the fate of nations". In 1925, the Archbishop of Naples claimed an earthquake on the Amalfi Coast was due to God's anger at these new shorter skirts.

Much to the probable delight of that archbishop, and in a way that Taylor could have predicted, hemlines fell again in 1929, as the stock markets crashed and the Great Depression began. The party was over. The 30s gave way to long, dramatic dresses, while 40s fashion was blighted by the rationing of another war, during which some women abandoned skirts completely for overalls and trousers that were more suited to the factory jobs that had previously been occupied by men. With Dior's New Look and its yards and yards of fabric unveiled in 1947, a new era was announced. The designer wanted "clothes with rounded shoulders, full feminine busts, and willowy waists above enormous spreading skirts," he wrote in 1954. The 50s saw Dior's calf-length designs become the norm – only to be disrupted with the arrival of Quant and friends, as a new decade began.

Circling back to the late 60s, and the mini – once a way for young women to mark themselves out from their mothers – was now worn by mothers; it was worn by almost all women. Its exact opposite, the maxi skirt, a floor-length design championed by the growing hippy movement, appeared around 1967. Rather than an "up", youthful energy, this mood – one that continued into the 70s – was languid and bohemian. Clothes were made for lounging around getting stoned, not dancing all night at a mod club.

Shorter skirts meant more scandal: as this photograph
demonstrates, young women wore them anyway

Sexy, tough and in charge:
Tina Turner's 80s take on the miniskirt

If the 70s passed in soft focus with the wafty layers to match, the edges were sharpened again in the 80s, with another economic boom. As Taylor could have once again predicted, the miniskirt was back. This time it came with a tougher – and sexier – attitude. Think Tina Turner in leather, Whitney Houston in a pink tube minidress or Melanie Griffith as the power-dressing Tess McGill in 1988's *Working Girl*. The miniskirt grew up in the 80s. In her memoir *Clothes... and Other Things That Matter*, ex-editor of *Vogue* Alexandra Shulman describes it as central to the wardrobe of career women at this time: "We were going to stride forth with our legs on display. Legs that were taking us places."[13] The mini was a way to show off shapely legs, but, like the boardroom-friendly shift dress now subtly shows off a yoga-honed physique, alpha women used it to say they can have it all. The aspiration for women in the 80s? As Tess McGill says: "a head for business and a bod for sin."

"MY ANGLE WAS IRONY"

WRITING IN 1969, James Laver opined: "It seems likely that what we are witnessing today is an *irreversible* wave of female emancipation, and if this is so, we may expect it to have a profound effect upon the clothes women wear."[14] In the modern era, you would have to say Laver was right. By the time I came of age in the late 90s, the mini had had its profound effect. It was now just something that women wore. You might wear it one day, a long slip dress the next, and a pair of Levi's the day after that.

But, still, the mini stood out. I remember chipping in with a couple of friends to buy a salmon-pink glittery number. With the exposure of so much leg came a certain level of defiance. Somehow, perhaps because of the 80s moment that came before it, a miniskirt was a way to say that you were a grown woman even if, like me, you were far from it. It meant poise, worldliness and independence – three qualities I only aspired to. Wearing a miniskirt let me try them on for size.

Me and my friends – cisgender young women growing up in liberal inner-city families – took the freedom to choose to dress in a sexy (or not) way for granted. It was for ourselves, rather than to appeal to any male gaze, or that was the theory. This reflected the place miniskirts had in popular culture. Cher Horowitz, the sassy heroine of 1995's *Clueless* – still one of my favourite films of all time – wears them almost constantly, but as a fashion statement rather than a way to seduce. The Spice Girls took the mini to the pop charts, and paired it with Girl Power and a dollop of mischief. The band often wore miniskirts – Posh's little black number, Baby's frilly slip, Ginger's knicker-baring Union Jack dress (which later sold for £41,000) – but they came with slogans like "Silence is golden but shouting is fun" rather than any bedroom eyes.

At the same time as the Spice Girls had their zig-a-zig-ah, the mini-with-attitude was gaining ground in subcultural dressing. Drawing on the heritage of punk (Vivienne Westwood had invented the Mini-Crini, from which a million puffballs spawned, in 1985), women on the riot grrrl scene made the mini part of their style. Zines were full of miniskirted figures, while Bikini Kill and Bratmobile stalked the stage in miniskirts and boots. The tampon-throwing L7 and Sonic Youth's frankly kick-ass Kim Gordon followed. And then there was the questionably titled "Kinderwhore" look, which saw Babes in Toyland and Hole subvert the saccharine femininity of frilly little-girl dresses they bought in thrift stores by wearing them with ripped tights and running eye make-up. "I didn't do the Kinderwhore thing because I thought I was so hot," Love told *Rolling Stone* in 1994. "When I started, it was a *What Ever Happened to Baby Jane?* thing ... My angle was irony."

*Geri Halliwell at the 1997 Brit Awards: bringing Girl
Power – and a flash of knickers – to the miniskirt story*

Less than 10 years on from *Working Girl*, the miniskirt was also a
part of the workwear wardrobe. Ally McBeal and her lawyer pals,
the descendants of Tess McGill, were dressed in miniskirt suits.
Rachel Green in *Friends* wore a miniskirt whether she was working as
a waitress or a merchandising manager at Ralph Lauren. And *Bridget
Jones's Diary*, Helen Fielding's 1996 bestseller, saw a miniskirt become
central to the plot – when Bridget's gets noticed by her boss Daniel
Cleaver. "You appear to have forgotten your skirt," he writes on still-
new-fangled instant messenger. "As I think is made perfectly clear in
your contract of employment, staff are expected to be fully dressed at
all times." No spoiler alert necessary. Most of us know how advances
like that usually end.

While Daniel Cleaver's behaviour would probably be dismissed
as workplace harassment now, Love's irony angle was huge by the

late 90s. This mood could be credited with the trend for young women choosing to dabble in porn aesthetics in the name of fashion – it felt acceptable, even clever, when accessorized with a wink. I remember the Playboy bunny as a popular tattoo choice, pink PVC as clubbing gear and S&M imagery in Ellen von Unwerth shoots. The mini was central here – because as well as being a feminist object, it has its place in male fantasies. Paris Hilton, Nicole Richie, Christina Aguilera and Britney Spears all wore skirts that skimmed their buttocks – sometimes paired with corsets or even a whip. If, in the 60s, the miniskirt's primary function was to signal female independence, young women 30 years later liked this history but were also keen to bring sexy back. With the broad brushstrokes of gender equality assumed to be in the bag, the decision to wear something straight out of the sex-shop playbook was seen as a "cool girl", sexually emancipated thing to do.

In 2005, writer Ariel Levy questioned this, popularizing the phrase "female chauvinist pigs" to describe this trend for "women who make sex objects of other women and of ourselves".[15] "'Raunchy' and 'liberated' are not synonyms," she wrote in her book, *Feminist Chauvinist Pigs*, asking if "this bawdy world of boobs and gams we have resurrected reflects how far we've come, or how far we have left to go."[16]

The idea of the mini as feminist statement, as seen in riot grrrl, still had its place. Luella Bartley switched career from fashion journalist to designer in 1999 with her label, Luella. In collections that referenced everything from The Clash to graffiti, skirt length was almost always short. "Even if I start a collection off knee length, the night before the show it has all been cut back to where it belongs," she wrote in her 2010 book, *Luella's Guide to English Style*. "VOTES FOR WOMEN!! LEGS OUT!!"[17] Various style icons emerged who agreed wholeheartedly and expressed this mainly through combining miniskirts with bovver boots and ripped fishnets: see Agyness Deyn, Alice Dellal and more.

THE LENGTH AND BREADTH

IN THE DIGITAL ERA, the idea of women owning their sexuality and choosing to show their bodies, as they did with minis in the 60s, has been taken to a new levels. This is perhaps exemplified by Emily Ratajkowski, the model and actor most famous for appearing in her knickers in the "Blurred Lines" video, and her 27 million Instagram followers. For Ratajkowski – a card-carrying feminist who has been papped reading Levy's memoir – the freedom to post that selfie, or wear something like a miniskirt, to be sexy if she feels like it, is evidence female empowerment has succeeded. In a 2019 essay published by *Harper's Bazaar*, she wrote, "I'm just making the point that women can and should be able to wear or represent themselves however they want, whether it's in a burka or a string bikini." She gives some examples: "I feel powerful when I'm feeling myself, and sometimes feeling myself means wearing a miniskirt. Sometimes it means wearing a giant hoodie and sweats … That's just me, in that moment."

Lizzo, a rare plus-size pop star, who has become an icon of the body positivity movement, probably agrees. She is as likely to wear a miniskirt as she is, on the cover of *Rolling Stone* in 2020, to be covered only in strategically placed flowers. Unlike Ratajkowski, who conforms to every parameter of what a supposedly conventionally attractive woman looks like, Lizzo is regularly criticized for what she wears. Her response? She is "good as hell". Taking to Instagram after she wore a dress exposing her thong to a basketball game, she was unapologetic – and, a little more forcefully than Ratajkowski, encourages fans to take a similar stance. "Who I am, and the essence of me, and the things that I choose to do as a grown-ass woman, can inspire you to do the same," she wrote.

Even with a Lizzo pep talk, though, not all women will have the confidence to wear a miniskirt now. As women age, that "right" to wear something like a miniskirt gets called into question. According to a Debenhams survey conducted in 2009, women should be wearing miniskirts only up to the age of 40. Another survey from 2016 found 39 too old. I can attest that this persistent age limit subtext around the miniskirt is pernicious. I tend to keep them to holidays where I feel more free of judgement.

Luckily for me, as I have grown older, the midi skirt has grown in fashionability. This is now the most common skirt length in my wardrobe – I have, at last count, 22 variations. I am far from alone. *The Guardian* introduced the over-the-knee style in 2013 as "the sleeper hit of the summer", quoting sales of the style on Asos as up by 200 per cent. By 2018, Net-a-Porter said the midi accounted for the largest proportion of skirt sales with the retailer, commenting that they "don't see that stopping" any time soon. There have even been midis with waiting lists – Whistles's Carrie pleated skirt back in 2011, the suede Marks & Spencer midi in 2015, and the Réalisation Par Naomi leopard slip skirt in 2019. Thanks to its versatility, relative newness, the fact society gives it a free pass across age, and even the rise of modest fashion, the midi is now ubiquitous where the mini once was.

So what does wearing a miniskirt mean in the twenty-first century? Both everything, and nothing at all. Miniskirts are still popular – in 2019, Asos said searches were up by over 100 per cent. Stand on a busy street on a sunny day and you might see 10 miniskirts in as little as an hour. The development of women's rights in the lifetime of the mini allows most young women in the West to just wear it, just as they can now vote or have a job. But the sexism inherent in society can be revealed with a woman's legs. Because even if she is wearing the miniskirt without thought – even if she is owning her sexuality, as she did in the 60s, as Lizzo recommends –

men still feel they have permission to objectify women in miniskirts on the street, every day. That's why the mini can never entirely escape comment, or controversy. Even now.

Over the past 10 years, a miniskirt ban was attempted in Castellammare di Stabia in Italy, and one succeeded in the offices of Southampton City Council. The mayor of the Italian town said the decision was to "facilitate better civil coexistence", echoing the breakdown-in-society rhetoric now dating back to the 20s. Similar bans have been threatened in Uganda. In Kenya, the Embu County Assembly banned them in 2020. The wearing of a miniskirt has seen a woman ending up in court in Zambia. And then there's that age-old idea: clothes as a way of women "asking for it". In 2013, a restaurant owner in Colombia suggested a woman was raped in his parking lot because she was wearing a miniskirt. In 2020, Ratajkowski accused photographer Jonathan Leder of sexually assaulting her in 2012. Leder hit back with the same old – now very tired – rhetoric: "You do know who we are talking about right? This is the girl that ... bounced around naked in the Robin Thicke video at that time. You really want someone to believe she was a victim?"

For the daughters and granddaughters of those 1968 feminists, the new wave of activists crowding London's streets for the Women's March and calling out everyday sexism online, the mini works as a wearable placard against such misogyny. The Colombian case caused a protest in Bogotá, with women wearing miniskirts in solidarity. This echoes the worldwide SlutWalk movement. Since 2011, women have united for marches across the world against sexual violence, wearing their "sluttiest" outfits. The miniskirt, as you can imagine, is a popular choice. Now worn by women for more than 50 years, it might be a given, but it is also an expression of women's freedom to wear what they want, when they want, how they want and at whatever age they want. Thinking about it like that, maybe I'll wear one tomorrow.

HOW TO WEAR
THE MINISKIRT NOW

Make like Mary and combine with a boot

The queen of the miniskirt is still the source of tips – even 50 years later. Quant wore hers with white knee-length boots, the kind that are enjoying a bit of a renaissance. Experiment with colours to bring that 60s feel up to date.

Practise your poses

We live in the era of social media, so getting that posture right in a miniskirt can make or break a look – after all, if you haven't taken a selfie, have you even worn an outfit? Take inspiration from your miniskirt idol, whether that's a 60s Twiggy, 80s Tina or modern-day Lizzo.

Tights are your friend

With more leg on display, you can make your tights part of your look too. Quant loved a pair of brightly coloured tights – introducing them to her clothing range in 1973 – so feel free to go for a mustard yellow, or a Billie Eilish green. It certainly brightens up the average winter weekday.

Find your length

From the 00s micro-mini to the 60s mid-thigh design, miniskirts vary wildly in length. The most important thing? Finding the one you're comfortable with. That way, you'll be striding forth with the best of them.

Different day, different mini

These days, there are enough minis to wear a different one every day of the year. A-line, ruffled, bright, black, PVC, denim and more. Take advantage of the miniskirt as a modern classic. Your take comes with what you wear with it – trainers, heels, sweatshirt or blouse. You decide.

NEED TO KNOW

- No one knows who first designed the miniskirt – it could have been André Courrèges, John Bates or Mary Quant. What is clear is that Quant popularized it. She was her own best model – the 60s answer to Victoria Beckham. She even wore a mini to collect her OBE in 1966.

- Versions of the mini existed before it was the mini – in ancient Egypt, in sci-fi comics and, of course, on schoolgirls. Rolling the waistband of school skirts isn't new. Teenagers did it back in the 60s, Twiggy and Quant included.

- After centuries of long skirts in the West, women's legs were first revealed in the 20s. It caused something of an upset for an older generation of Victorians. And in 1925, the Archbishop of Naples claimed that an earthquake on the Amalfi Coast was due to God's anger at shorter skirts.

- Economist George Taylor came up with a theory called the hemline index – suggesting hemlines went up in times of prosperity, and down in times of hardship. It has worked so far – the 20s, the 60s, the 80s and the early 00s were all boom times when the mini dominated.

- The miniskirt might be the stuff of male fantasy, but it's also a feminist symbol, worn by those in the women's liberation movement in the 60s. This continues today – the mini is worn proudly on protests throughout the world and by women going about their business every day.

- It remains controversial. Over the last past 10 years, wearing a miniskirt could land a woman in court in Zambia, get her a fine in Italy and get her sent home if she worked for Southampton County Council. All the more reason to wear one.

THE JEANS

Andy Warhol wanted to die in them. Giorgio Armani described them as democratic. Diana Vreeland dubbed them the most beautiful things since the gondola.[1] On any given day, half of the world's population is wearing them. Where there is human civilization, there are almost always jeans.

I have 11 pairs. Bleached 1990s ones by Acne, red ones from Whistles, cropped boot-cut Topshop ones, high-waisted skinnies and two pairs of Levi's 501s – one new-ish, and a pair given to me by my stepmum ages ago. These are probably my favourite pair – and not just for sentimental reasons. The fact that these are Levi's 501s makes them highly prized. Though there are now an almost infinite variety of jeans, the 501 came first.

Jeans at work: Californian miners wearing hardwearing
trousers, still known as "waist overalls", in the 1880s

A TRUE ORIGINAL

AS AMERICAN AS APPLE PIE, Levi Strauss & Co was founded by
immigrants. Levi – or Loeb – Strauss emigrated to New York from
Bavaria in 1846, joining two of his half-brothers, who had a dry goods
business. Moving west with the gold rush, Strauss started his own dry
goods business in San Francisco in 1853. He sold everything from
handkerchiefs to blankets and "jean pants", the workwear trousers that
preceded the design we know as jeans.[2]

It was Jacob Davis, or Jacob Youphes, a Jewish tailor from Latvia,
who designed the first Levi's. Emigrating to the US in 1854, he settled
in Reno in 1868, opening a tailor's shop. Receiving a commission from

a woman to make a pair of hard-wearing trousers for her labourer husband, Davis reinforced his design with the metal rivets he used on horse blankets. The rivets evolved the jean pant into something new. With rivets on the corners of pockets where the trousers had most wear and tear, Davis's design stood up to the hard physical labour his customers performed every day. Realizing others were onto his idea, he needed a patent, but he didn't have the money to finance it. In 1872, he wrote to his denim supplier, Levi Strauss, suggesting they collaborate.

Strauss clearly knew a good idea when he saw it. On 20 May 1873, the duo were granted patent 139121 and, as the Levi's website puts it: "Blue jeans are born." These jeans – called "waist overalls" at the time – came with suspender buttons along the top, instead of belt loops. There was only one back pocket. The second one, so innate to the design we know, was not added until 1901. But, while other fashion items have changed beyond recognition, nineteenth-century jeans resemble the ones worn today.

Strauss and Davis sold their jeans at outlets targeting the growing population of labourers, gold miners and cowboys on the west coast. While there were other brands making jean pants, the duo's rivets helped them stand out. In 1890, Strauss and Davis's patent ended, and they began to market their jeans as 501s to stay distinctive in a soon-to-be crowded market. The Hudson Overall Company – now Wrangler – was founded in 1904 in North Carolina. Henry David Lee, in Kansas, had had a successful grocery business since 1889. In 1912, he branched out into workwear, including jeans.

Hard-wearing denim had by this point been used by working people for centuries – first in Europe. A twill made from cotton fibres, the "weft" (horizontal) white thread is woven together with two "warp" (vertical) threads dyed blue, forming the distinctive diagonal twill pattern, and the white reverse side. *Serge de Nîmes* was a cotton/wool mix that hailed from the French city, made in the 1500s. Denim itself might be a French product, or it could be British and called denim – as in *de Nîmes* – to make it sound more cosmopolitan. There was also a fustian wool/cotton blend from Genoa. It was called "jean" – possibly as a shortening of "Genoa" – by Brits; the word was in use by 1567 according to the *Oxford English Dictionary*.[3] Lord Byron ordered "white jean trowsers" from his tailor in 1812.[4]

The cotton that made denim came with dark connotations. In 1860, the US exported 3.8 million bales of cotton, and it was mostly picked by the approximately 4 million slaves in the country at the time. As such, the denim first sold in Strauss's shop could have been the product of slave labour. While largely founded in the years after slavery was abolished in 1865, the denim industry benefited from the production systems put in place by it, and the workforce would still have been poorer, minority groups. A lot of cotton – whether for denim or for T-shirts – was picked by impoverished Black sharecroppers. Levi's denim was manufactured by the Amoskeag Manufacturing Company in Manchester, New Hampshire, from 1873 until 1915. Employees at Amoskeag would have been white immigrant workers from Ireland, Germany and Canada. These were men, women – and sometimes children, as Lewis Hines's images from 1909 demonstrate – willing to work for lower wages.

Indigo, the shade we so associate with jeans and made from the plant of the same name, has its own backstory. It was used in Ancient Egypt – a robe in Tutankhamun's tomb was made of indigo-dyed cloth, and rich Romans would import the dye for a price 15 times the average daily wage.[5] The plant was spread in the US by white colonial transplant Elizabeth Lucas Pinckney. Born in Antigua, Pinckney moved to South Carolina as a teenager and managed one of her father's plantations in the 1740s. When her father sent her some indigo seeds, she successfully cultivated them, scaling up the production with slave labour. By 1754, South Carolina was exporting more than 454,000 kilograms of indigo each year. Indigo made sense for jeans when they were popularized. Here was a colour that looked durable, and a dye that took to the cotton well. At the end of the nineteenth century a version of synthetic indigo was invented, making uniform colour more possible.

New jeans, for a
new century

BY THE 1920S, CONSUMERS were calling jeans jeans, and they were part of workers' wardrobes.[6] Levi's were market leaders – in 1929, sales of their waist overalls accounted for 10–15 per cent of all workwear sales on the west coast.[7]

The term "blue collar" was first used by an Iowan newspaper in 1924, and *Slate* suggests this was due to the already-established connection between manual workers and blue jeans, chambray shirts and dungarees. There was also a new place to spot jeans – on cowboys in the movies. Gary Cooper can be seen in cuffed jeans in 1938's *The Cowboy and the Lady*, and for his breakout role in John Ford's 1939 *Stagecoach*, John Wayne wears 501s.

The 30s were the decade of the Great Depression, with nearly 15 million people out of work. As documented by photographers Dorothea Lange and Walker Evans, many of these poor men and women wore jeans, but they couldn't afford to buy new ones. Levi's 1932 sales were half of what they were in 1929.[8]

The shift of jeans from practical workwear to style statement began, as jeans brands began to court middle-class consumers. The jeans worn by movie stars helped, as did a fashion for all things rodeo – by 1940, 25,000 families a year visited dude ranches: Western-themed holiday parks for stressed-out middle classes to hike, fish and ride horses wearing jeans.[9] Jeans brands repositioned their product as an all-American clothing choice, worn by that all-American hero, the cowboy.

*Wearing the trousers: Katharine Hepburn didn't enjoy
being told what to do, hence her wearing jeans in the 30s*

With this new market, there was a new consumer: women. While poor women might have linked jeans to toil, the more privileged began to see them as modern, the kind of thing worn by independently minded movie stars like Marlene Dietrich and Katharine Hepburn. Hepburn's attachment to her jeans provoked much scandal in Hollywood. While she was working at RKO Pictures studios, her jeans were confiscated – presumably by studio heads hoping she would switch to a skirt. They were disappointed – Hepburn walked around in just her knickers until the jeans reappeared.

Levi's launched the first ever jeans for women, the Lady Levi's or 701s, in 1934. According to the brand, working women had been wearing men's jeans, and students at the women's colleges known as the Seven Sisters wore purposefully scruffy jeans as part of what Simone de Beauvoir called their "studied carelessness".[10] But making jeans for respectable women was controversial – any trousers were unusual, and these had added associations with both workers and non-conformists like Hepburn. Levi's used this to cleverly position jeans as a fashion-forward choice. In 1935, there was an advertising spread in *Vogue* with the playful title, "What! Overalls in Vogue?"

While the Depression had eased in the final years of the 30s, the US joined the Second World War in 1941. Jeans for women were seen differently again – they were now a practical and even patriotic choice. Rosie the Riveter – depicted by Norman Rockwell in denim dungarees on the front of *Life* magazine in 1943 – was *the* poster woman for denim. Studied carelessness was in.

Rebels – with or without causes

IT WAS THE 1950S, of course, when jeans changed fashion forever, as part of the uniform of the teenager, an age group acknowledged as distinct from children or adults for the first time. More independent, thanks to their own disposable income – a side effect of a booming post-war economy – they also had their own music, in rock'n'roll, and their own clothes.

Jeans, more widely available from the late 40s, became a way for American teens to distinguish themselves from the older generation. Clashing with a grown-up's idea of clothing as a way to signal success and respectability, jeans in this era may be the first incidence of people choosing to "dress down".

The cowboy connection was key, with cultural anthropologist Ted Polhemus calling him "the first universally acceptable Working-Class Hero".[11] The Beats, as modern outlaws in crumpled jeans, also had a part to play. Jack Kerouac's bestselling *On the Road* was published in 1957. William S Burroughs, looking back in 1969, wrote that the book and its author "was responsible for selling a million pairs of jeans".

But movie stars and musicians sold more – often wearing jeans with their partner-in-style, the white T-shirt: see *The Wild One* and *Rebel Without a Cause*, with James Dean in Lee jeans, white T-shirt and red blouson jacket. Levi's released black "Elvis Presley Jeans" for *Jailhouse Rock* in 1956. The take-up of jeans by rebellion's poster boys meant they were – like T-shirts – banned in schools for fear of juvenile delinquency. This only fuelled the fire. As James Sullivan writes in his cultural history of jeans: "Like mind-altering substances, premarital sex, or banned books, jeans were increasingly coveted *because* they were prohibited."[12]

As time went on, such controversy faded – and jeans rippled out to the rest of the family. Women were increasingly included; Levi's adverts from the 50s specifically targeted housewives, with the slogan "so smart, so practical". Women soon had their own celluloid icon too: Marilyn Monroe. First wearing them in *Clash by Night* in 1952, Monroe's real iconic denim moment came when she wore Levi's on a ranch in 1961's *The Misfits*. The connection between jeans and sex was born.

Young Americans weren't the only people adopting jeans. GIs were in Europe and Japan during and immediately after the Second World War, and they brought their jeans with them. As all things American became the last word in pop-culture cool across the globe, jeans were objects of desire, particularly for young working-class men. Marc Bolan was then a teenage modernist, the British subculture that evolved into the mods. He stole Levi's from a shop in Whitechapel. "It was great knowing we were only one of a few people in England who had them," he said in a later interview. "That was very funky."

Jeans were funky in Japan too. Now home to artisan denim and its own much sought-out jeans brands, they weren't commonly worn

*Jeans get political: denim as worn on the Stonewall
anniversary march in 1970*

in the country until after the war. First called "G-Pans", they were
sourced secondhand from markets and imported from the States.
They could cost up to half a month's salary.[13]

Behind the Iron Curtain, jeans were contraband. In East
Germany, "rivet pants" could see you get sent home from school.
Levi's and the like would have been posted as part of a "Western"
parcel from relatives on the other side or bought on the black
market. In 50s communist Russia, Western jeans signalled dangerous
"bourgeois" youth.

By the 60s, though, jeans were worn by young people who were
part of youthquakes around the world. They were a symbol of
tuning in and dropping out at Woodstock, worn by students in Paris
and Prague in 1968, and on protesters during LGBTQ+ liberation
marches post-Stonewall. As each movement emerged, so did its chosen
jean. The market flourished. Levi's sales reached over $100 million in
the decade. In 1971, 350 million pairs were sold.[14]

Nothing comes between her and her Calvins: a young
Brooke Shields brings sex appeal to the denim market

A BACK VIEW

THE FIRST DESIGNER JEAN could be traced back to a familiar name – that of Fred Segal. The man who later founded the department store began selling so-called hip-hugger jeans in Los Angeles, for $7.95, then a hefty sum of money for trousers that many still considered workwear.[15] Europe got involved in the late 1960s with Elio Fiorucci, a designer who took pop art and made it fashion by adding sex appeal. He launched the Buffalo 70s Jean in 1970, which the brand (relaunched in 2017) claims is the first skinny jean. It was prompted by Fiorucci's jet-set lifestyle and a trip to Ibiza. "He watched all the girls walk out the club in the morning with their jeans on, and they walked into the water," Stephen Schaffer, the brand's new co-owner, told me. "He thought: 'Look how amazing they look when they're wet.'"

By the mid-70s, Buffalos were worn far away from the White Isle – they could now be found in Manhattan, as disco fever hit. Their higher price tag and tighter fit did away with the workwear associations, and chimed with the glamour of the dancefloor. Their popularity got Fiorucci a namecheck in Sister Sledge's disco classic "He's the Greatest Dancer", and put them on the radar of other burgeoning fashion brands – particularly those specifically aimed at women. Working with marketing whizz Warren Hirsch, socialite Gloria Vanderbilt created her eponymous jeans brand in 1976, inspired by the fit of the Fiorucci's, but with her name on the back pocket. Consumers might not have been born with a trust fund or have Truman Capote on speed dial like Vanderbilt, but they could wear the jeans. They sold in their thousands.

Although it had less WASP pedigree, "Calvin Klein" appeared on the backs of jeans too. By 1979, the New York brand had shifted $70 million worth of women's jeans. The sex appeal was made explicit – and infamous – in 1980, with the Calvin Klein advert featuring a 15-year-old Brooke Shields and the line, "Do you know what comes between me and my Calvins? Nothing." Klein specified later that: "Jeans are sex."

Women's jeans in this era were about sex, yes, but in a way that felt more on the wearer's own terms than other items of clothing. A woman could dance all night in a pair of jeans without fear of men's hands creeping up her skirt. She could display her body, but also cover it. She was in control – or it seemed that way, anyway. In fact, the decision to wear jeans – as with the decision to wear a miniskirt – has been used against women. In 1998, a ruling at the Italian Supreme Court overturned a rape conviction because the victim was wearing jeans. The court argued she must have provided consent because "it is a fact of common experience that it is nearly impossible to slip off tight jeans". As with the miniskirt, jeans were subsequently taken up by feminists as an item of solidarity for abused women – female members of parliament came to work wearing jeans the day after the decision; since 1999, Denim Day in April has campaigned for women to have the right to wear jeans free of harassment.

The eroticism of a body encased in jeans wasn't limited to the heteronormative world. The "Castro clone" look gained ground in the 70s in San Francisco's Castro district, an area popular with the LGBTQ+ community, and was taken up by gay men globally. As fashion historian Shaun Cole writes, this look styled itself upon society's typical image of white masculinity: the working man. Wearers of the style "adopted the most masculine dress signifiers they could find – work boots, tight Levi's, plaid shirts".[16] They then hit the gym for the muscular body type to match.

An alternative, less fixed, dress code was found on the disco dancefloor. If the scene provided women with a (relatively) safe space, New York clubs like The Loft, 12 West, Studio 54 and Paradise Garage – famed door policies aside – also welcomed young LGBTQ+ people and people of colour. Bill Bernstein, who photographed the scene, describes it as "a haven for acceptance and inclusion."[17] Tight jeans were a democratic dancefloor stalwart. Comfortable, sexy and robust enough for an all-nighter, they allowed their wearer to get lost in music.

"EASY, CASUAL"

BY THE 80S, JEANS were commonplace – they had even entered politics, with Jimmy Carter, the former peanut farmer, wearing them to great humblebrag effect in his 1976 campaign. They could be status symbols, they could be about sex, or they could signal membership of a certain tribe. In the wake of disco, the homoerotic overtones of denim would not have been lost on Bruce Springsteen. He featured Levi's on the cover of *Born in the USA* in 1984, an album that heavily critiques ideas of American patriotism and what it means to be a man. Then 501 fever occurred in 1985, with Nick Kamen, in a 1950s launderette, stripping down to his boxers. Sales went up 800 per cent. But the casually sexy vibe associated with jeans was soon to come into stark contrast with the public mood. The same year that Kamen

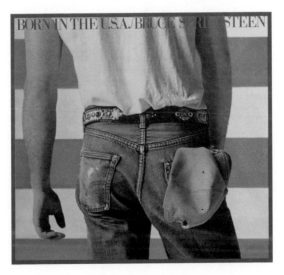

*American boy: Bruce Springsteen's seminal album
cover, with its iconic Levi's jeans*

smouldered on screens, Rock Hudson died of AIDS and cases spread worldwide. The anything-goes freedom found amongst jeans-clad crowds at night clubs in the late 70s was well and truly over – with the fear of HIV sobering up the scene.

Meanwhile, in the fashion world, Anna Wintour put a model in jeans and a Christian Lacroix jacket on her first ever cover of *Vogue* in 1988. Being more used to ballgowns, the printers called to check it was the right image. Writing about the cover in 2012, Wintour said, "It looked easy, casual, a moment that had been snapped on the street, which it had been, and which was the whole point." Indeed, jeans were now a mainstay on streets across the world – see the young people photographed sitting on the demolished Berlin Wall in 1989: they were almost all wearing jeans.

Ragged, baggy and feathered

GRUNGE – HITTING THE mainstream in 1991 with Nirvana's *Nevermind* – was once dismissed by Jean Paul Gaultier as "nothing more than the way we dress when we have no money". Kurt Cobain's jeans certainly paid tribute to his blue-collar upbringing: they were ripped and patched, and worn defiantly for everything from gigs to award ceremonies. Fans replicated the styles. I remember wearing an old pair of Levi's, with a checked shirt and Dr Martens, almost as often as I listened to *Nevermind*.

If disco had seen jeans taken up by people of colour in a niche scene, hip-hop increased their popularity. Jamel Shabazz's late-70s images of the burgeoning hip-hop scene show young people of colour in New York wearing straight jeans. As hip-hop grew, so did the circumference of the average jean leg. From the 80s, the cuts were loosened – with stars like Snoop Dogg, Wu-Tang Clan and Biggie Smalls all wearing jeans several sizes too big and low on the waist. It was the start of a style now called "saggin". Some say this trend came from prison – with inmates not allowed to wear belts – and made its way to the outside. Others have connected it to the wide-fit zoot suits in the 40s. Another theory is that the oversized look is designed to challenge the status quo and visually arrest the viewer.

Brands began to cater to this market. Designer Karl Kani made baggy jeans from around 1991, commenting, "Black men do not like fitted jeans", and April Walker founded Walker Wear the same year. Rappers including Tupac Shakur, Biggie, LL Cool J and Dr Dre wore Kani's and Walker's jeans. By 1997, Kani's sales reached around $50 million.[18] Tommy Hilfiger – who started out selling secondhand jeans – shrewdly realized there was money to be made out of the XXXL shapes, as hip-hop style spread to affluent and suburban communities, and he changed the fit of his clothes accordingly. In 1996, his was the number one clothing brand on the New York Stock Exchange.

The late 90s also saw the growth of independent jeans brands. I remember buying a pair of Earl jeans on a trip to the States. A *New York Times* article from 2001 calls them "the brand of choice among members of the fashion flock", the people I was desperate to join. The second generation of designer jeans arrived, putting denim on the catwalk for good. Tom Ford's $3,000 feathered jeans from 1999 were ordered by Gwyneth Paltrow, Lil' Kim and Madonna, and jeans were now appropriate for the red carpet. The year 2001 was key: Stella McCartney wore jeans to the *Vanity Fair* Oscars party, there was the much-meme'd Justin Timberlake and Britney Spears in their quadruple denim at the American Music Awards, and Destiny's Child chose matching hipsters and cropped tops for an MTV event.

The 00s saw these hipster jeans become the norm for women, eventually sitting only just above the pubic bone. To be avoided?

*Down low: Destiny's Child model the noughties hipster
jean – and requisite midriff section – in 2001*

The so-called "muffin top", where flesh spills over the low waistband. Thanks to hipsters, women had gained a new body part to be derided.

The never-ending trend

AS JEANS' WAISTBANDS went lower, the legs began to narrow to something very familiar: the skinny jean. Now a standard, skinny jeans have actually been around for a long time – Levi's had stretch in them from the 60s, there were disco jeans like Fiorucci's Buffalos, and the drainpipes worn by punk bands like The Ramones. It's possible Trash and Vaudeville, the New York punk store, popularized them from the late 70s. They can also be traced back to Rachael Fleming, the costume designer of *Trainspotting* in 1996. "[She] basically invented skinny jeans for men," said Ewen Bremner, who played Spud in the film. "She would take women's jeans and restitch them, or men's jeans and cut them apart and restitch them. That was down to her, that whole movement!"

It was The Ramones who inspired The Strokes. In turn, the 00s New York band, with their skinny battered denim choices, in turn inspired a generation. Other endorsements from the indie style playbook helped. See Kate Moss in her grey skinnies, her then-boyfriend Pete Doherty and bandmates in The Libertines, the Yeah Yeah Yeahs, Bloc Party and the white-jeaned Johnny Borrell in Razorlight. Hedi Slimane, then the designer at Dior Homme, brought skinny jeans – and boys in bands – to the catwalk. Topshop launched the skinny low-rise Baxter in 2005 and sold 18,000 every week in the first nine months they were on sale. This popularity meant that they quite quickly lost their edge: politicians, parents, babies – everyone and anyone starting wearing them. By 2013, *The Guardian* published an article titled "Skinny jeans: the fashion trend that refuses to die". *Vogue* were "calling time on skinny jeans" by 2016. And yet they remain. The style accounted for 38 per cent of the women's denim market in 2020.

If the mainstream narrative of the 00s was around skinny jeans, those saggin jeans worn by some young people of colour in the US were the subjects of controversy, due to the fact that jeans were now worn so low that buttocks in underwear were fully visible. "Not since the zoot suit has a style been greeted with such strong disapproval," wrote the *New York Times* in 2007. As in the 50s, jeans became symbols of criminality – but this was more than getting told off at school. A city in Louisiana instituted a law that wearing jeans this way could mean a six-month jail term. Others followed. Shreveport in Louisiana didn't repeal its law until 2019, when a Black man, Anthony Childs, was fatally shot after a police chase apparently motivated by his saggin jeans. Similar profiling has occurred in Berlin with Picaldi jeans, popular with young working-class men and demonized as a symbol of dangerous and idle youth.[19] While jeans are a safe choice for many through their ubiquity, that doesn't hold for all. Some styles, worn by some people, remain a perceived threat.

A RIPPLE EFFECT

EVEN BEFORE THEY get to consumers, jeans make their mark on people and the planet – often far away from where they are worn. As with T-shirts, the cotton that makes jeans requires a lot of water and uses a lot of pesticides.[20] The rivets that Strauss and Davis were so proud of now make jeans unrecyclable and the Pearl River system in China is polluted because of jeans production.[21] Egypt, India and Uzbekistan are among the countries that use child labour to pick the cotton that makes our jeans.[22] Factory workers in Bangladesh often earn around $38 a month, less than half of the living wage in the country,[23] and workers in Turkey have developed respiratory problems due to sandblasting techniques used to give a distressed finish.[24] A report by the Global Slavery Index in 2018 put clothes as the second biggest product group using slave labour, particularly across African and Asian countries, with product imported into G20 countries. If half the world on any given day are wearing jeans, it's likely that people somewhere are suffering to get them made.

But even with these grisly facts, the appetite for jeans remains, with the global market valued in 2018 at $66.2 billion. Even if that figure was hit by the lockdown of 2020, when homeworking saw sweatpants emerge as the trouser of choice, and Levi's sales drop by 62 per cent in the second quarter, jeans remain a central part of what most of us wear. The trends ebb and flow, and come from both society and the fashion world. A focus on the environment has meant growth in sustainably minded brands like MUD and ELV, while Levi's 2020 collaboration with Denim Tears' Tremaine Emory addresses the history of cotton and Black women in the South, like both of Emory's grandmothers. As for shapes, boyfriend jeans, mom jeans, dad jeans and kick flares may yet oust the skinny, while the *Daily Mail* recently reported the unsettling news that the hipster is making a comeback. For denim nerds, Japanese selvedge jeans are the holy grail. They can cost up to $2,000 a pair, thanks to specialist craftspeople weaving on vintage looms, natural dyes and the use of raw denim. These are the antithesis of artificially distressed designs found on the high street. Aficionados turn up the hems to see the red thread of selvedge, a mark of those old looms, and wash them only once a year.

Jeans are not treated with such reverence by most of us, though. They are what we wear when we can't think of anything else; for dates, for work, for working from home, for errands, for clubs, for everything. We take our jeans for granted, but maybe we shouldn't. Maybe, whenever we next pull on a pair of jeans, we should instead, as Ted Polhemus once said, "remind ourselves how revolutionary they once were".[25]

HOW TO WEAR JEANS NOW

Go vintage
Not only will you do your bit for the planet, but you'll get that distressed and worn-in look for real. That brings a distinct feeling of satisfaction when getting dressed.

The classics are still the best
Sure, most brands do jeans. But for the real thing, there's nothing better than the original brands: the Levi's, the Lees, the Wranglers. If you listen closely, you can still hear the whisper of the mountain range.

Find your reference
Of which there are a fair few. See Katharine Hepburn scandalizing 30s Hollywood, James Dean in *Rebel Without a Cause*, Beyoncé circa 2001. This is the way to discover the jeans that you want to buy into. Like their style? Then you'll probably like their jeans.

Try loads of them on
Yeah, bad news, but you'll find the ones that actually suit you when you have despaired over approximately 72 other pairs. It's the only way to know if you are a boot-cut, straight leg or – yes, they still exist – a skinny-jean person.

Go to Japan
New bucket-list entry. Kojima is the place that denim heads flock to – where there is "jeans street" (actually four streets) with nearly 40 shops to buy jeans. Make the journey and come back with jeans to impress even the biggest denim snobs.

NEED TO KNOW

- On 20 May 1873, jeans began their journey to your wardrobe. Levi Strauss and Jacob Davis were granted patent 139121 for riveted work pants, or "waist overalls" as they were then called. They were swiftly adopted by miners, farmers and more for manual work.

- Denim dates back much further – to France, Italy and England. The word "jean" has been traced back to Italy, possibly as a British shortening of "Genoa". Denim itself is now thought to have first been made either in France, or in England.

- Cowboys are key to why we wear jeans – they bring the authenticity of the Western. John Wayne, Gary Cooper and others wore them out on the range, and partially inspired James Dean and Marlon Brando to do the same. Thanks to cinema, teenagers adopted the symbol of rebels without a cause in the 1950s.

- Jeans became shorthand for sex appeal in the 70s, whether on the dancefloor at Studio 54 or in San Francisco's Castro district. As Calvin Klein himself said: "Jeans are sex."

- The skinny jean is still the shape of our time. Rising in fashionability in the early 00s, it remains 20 years later, making the shape one of the longest trends ever. Boyfriend jeans, mom jeans, dad jeans and kick flares are threatening to oust them though.

Tracey Panek
Historian, Levi Strauss & Co

Soon after Tracey Panek was appointed official in-house historian at Levi's, she met a woman called Barbara Hunter Kepon. Hunter Kepon, in her 80s, had something very interesting to show Panek – a pair of Levi's 501s that dated back to the 1880s. "She lived in the Los Angeles area, and she and her friends as teenagers went into a mine and found a pile of jeans," explains Panek. "She pulled out one of them, found the two-horses trademark in the inside pocket and realized they were a pair of Levi's."

Hunter Kepon wore jeans to high school, in the 40s, when few women wore trousers, let alone jeans. "It would have been very unusual, but she was kind of ahead of her time," says Panek.

Panek has a job title of dreams, but she is a measured and low-key presence – a bit like the kind school librarian who quietly slips you a book to change your life, with a barely discernible twinkle.

This story is just one of many she has at her disposal – along with boxes of old Levi's products, going almost as far back as the foundation of the company in 1873. Another story details the discovery of a 100-year-old ripped and shredded – but recognizable – pair of 201s, the 501's budget cousins, in the Klondike area of Canada. With its history as a Gold Rush area, it's likely they were worn by a miner. And there's another rebellious woman in pants. "Viola Bedford was a teacher in central California," details Panek. "She bought her Levi's in the 30s and wore them while she was going to university. We think what she had was a prototype of what would become the Lady Levi's. That was a really amazing discovery. We learned all about Viola and her story, not just her pants."

Panek says the wider context is what makes the story of jeans illuminating: "You can follow a lot of trends, cultural trends, in what's happened to the blue jean and how they have been worn over time." Levi's is the oldest existing jeans brand, so their history also chronicles broader historical moments including the migration of immigrant workers (the two-horses logo on the back of the jeans was designed to be recognizable without being able to speak English), the women's movement (the introduction of women's jeans in 1934), the Second World War (GIs took Levi's overseas) and the rise of the teenager demographic. "It's during this era, when movies like *The Wild One* come out, you have schools banning students from wearing blue jeans. And of course what do they want to wear? Just what they aren't meant to."

Asked why she thinks the jeans have continued to be integral to youth culture and marginalized groups – ranging from rockers to mods to the LGBTQ+ community – Panek theorizes that there are several factors. "They are definitely a blank canvas for self-expression," she says. "Their roots make them even more appealing – they began as this workwear garment and the kind of clothing you want to have, to fit in, with a wide variety of groups." She points to the patchwork trend in the 60s where hippies would embroider peace signs on their jeans, and the hanky code, a practice among gay men in the 70s and 80s who used coloured handkerchiefs in their back pockets to indicate their sexual preferences.

Even if the past is her speciality, Panek doesn't imagine the future will be much different when it comes to jeans. "I love the quote that Yves Saint Laurent once said, that he wished he invented blue jeans because they have all these elements he loves – expression, modesty, sex appeal and simplicity," she says. "It's a timeless garment that has worked and continues to work for generations."

THE BALLET FLAT

I was late to ballet. At six, around the age little girls typically fall for the tutus and tights, I was indifferent and soon abandoned the "good toes, naughty toes" classes my mum had enrolled me in. Instead, aged 12, when everyone else had moved on to frenemies and schoolyard crushes, I fell for ballet. Hard.

Every Thursday, I would head to the basement of my local library where poor Maria, my ballet teacher, would try in vain to get me to do a successful plié, let alone a pirouette. Despite a distinct lack of talent, I researched entry to the Royal Ballet School, I read everything I could about Margot Fonteyn, I made my sister sit through a regional production of *Giselle*. And – cliché that I was – I dreamed tirelessly of going en pointe in a pair of baby-pink satin ballet shoes, the kind with ribbons that snake up the ankle.

FULL OF GRACE

MUCH TO THE DISAPPOINTMENT of my 12-year-old self, I never did go en pointe – let alone become a prima ballerina. This makes me like most women. Real ballerinas are unicorns of our culture; people for the rest of us to marvel at, to admire at a distance, fantasy women found in music boxes. But, if most of us will never be ballerinas, we do wear their shoes. Or a version of them, anyway. The shoes I wore in that library basement were ballet slippers, the flat leathery ones, in a pale pink, with a little string bow on the front. These are, broadly speaking, the model for a shoe that can now be found at the bottom of a commuter's handbag, on the feet of both Melania Trump and Alexa Chung, and on flower girls at weddings. At best a pretty alternative to a high heel, at worst a mundane A-to-B solution, the ballet flat is an every-shoe. But it's the alliance with the ballerina that makes it endure.

LEARNING THE STEPS

BALLET CAN BE TRACED back to Italy in the sixteenth century, and the root of the word comes from the Italian word *ballare*, "to dance". Catherine de' Medici – a kind of It girl of her day – brought a form of the dance to France when she married the future King Henry II in 1533. At first, due to ornate and heavy outfits, headdresses and heeled dress shoes, it consisted of slow ceremonial movements.

Aristocrats performed these early ballets at court. King Louis XIV was particularly keen. He gained his nickname, the Sun King, thanks to performing as the Sun god Apollo in a ballet at the age of 15. By the 1680s, trained dancers began to perform, and in theatres rather

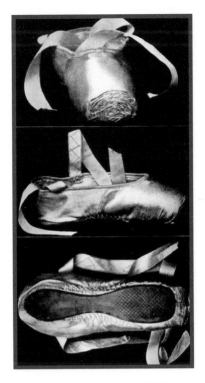

As worn by a swan: Anna Pavlova's ballet shoes,
complete with toe darning and ankle ribbons

than at court. Women began to dance the female roles from 1681, but with dancers still wearing heeled shoes.

Marie Camargo changed that. Making her debut at the Paris Opera in 1726, she took on jumping steps previously performed by male dancers and adjusted what she wore so she could move more easily. She raised skirts to calf length, and began to wear form-fitting "drawers", an eighteenth-century precursor to the snug tights dancers wear today. Crucially, she removed the heels from those dancing shoes and danced in the kind of ballet slippers we would recognize. French dancers – presumably fortified with incredible pain thresholds – performed a version of en pointe in these shoes. If a pair from 1860 is anything to go by, they were merely darned to reinforce the toe.

While Camargo's name is not now known outside dance circles, Anna Pavlova remains the epitome of a ballerina more than 100 years after she first danced *The Dying Swan* in 1905. She also has a starring role in the story of ballet shoes. With very high arches, Pavlova reinforced the toe of her shoes and added leather midsoles, leading to the design of modern pointe shoes. Other dancers followed her lead. The pointe shoes we recognize, made using layers of fabric glued to a hard "block" at the toe, were developed by Freed in London and Capezio in New York in the 1920s.

Dance and style began to gel in Pavlova's era. She danced with the Ballets Russes, Sergei Diaghilev's company, with costumes by designers including Coco Chanel and Sonia Delaunay. In 1920, an illustration of two en pointe ballerinas covered *Vogue*. By the 30s, "balletomania" hit. The dance style became the aspirational fodder of fashion magazines. A *Vogue* editorial in 1935 describes ballet as possessing "a glamour, a romantic pungency, unsurpassed by any other form in that it excites the eye and the ear simultaneously and equally."[1] Noel Streatfeild's novel *Ballet Shoes* was published the following year and became required reading for children dreaming of tutus and tights.

It was in the 40s when ballet style – and ballet flats – crossed over from something strictly for the stage to something for all women to wear. The beginnings of this can be traced back to the innovative former dancer and influential magazine editor Diana Vreeland, who had a knack for the new. In the July 1941 issue of *Harper's Bazaar*, then edited by Vreeland, black dancing slippers are featured as shoes to wear on the street. "Now is the time to tie up our ankles," the text read. "The new ballet shoes may be worn at any time day or night."[2]

Vreeland herself was a model, wearing them with white shirts and bold jewellery. The same year, Valentina, an outspoken designer and former dancer who dressed stars like Katharine Hepburn, was also photographed in them.

The Second World War had a hand in the ballet slipper's new fashionability. Shoe rationing came into effect in the US in 1943, with the use of leather limited. Ballet shoes, however, were exempt from legislation. Claire McCardell, part of the US's first wave of innovative designers working with sportswear, collaborated with Capezio, who had been making shoes for dancers since 1887. Possibly encouraged by Vreeland, the designer put models in ballet flats for a collection in 1944 and claimed the trend as her own. Even McCardell was surprised by the take-up by urban women, though. In a fashion anthology from the 70s, a *Life* magazine editor quotes the designer saying, "I meant them for the home or the country club, not the subway."

The ballet flat worked for fashion in the US during this period, when function was the buzzword for a new generation of women designing for women. "Thanks to the creative output of mid-century female fashion designers and the influence of ballerinas, a unique American design idiom arose," wrote Patricia Mears, Deputy Director of the Museum at the Fashion Institute of Technology, in the catalogue for 2019 exhibition *Ballerina: Fashion's Modern Muse*.[3] Of course, this influence also provided another prism through which fashion could refract an idolization of a thin white woman – see the ballerina spinning inside a child's music box.

By 1944, *Vogue* deemed that ballet flats should "no longer confine their talents to the stage".[4] And in 1949, Capezio flats were on the cover. Unlike the miniskirt, which put itself at the heart of gender politics, the ballet flat was not feminist per se. These were shoes that, instead, gently acknowledged changes in women's lives post-war. They felt modern because they allowed a more active lifestyle, but

Incorporating Vanity Fair
May 15, 1949
Price 50 Cents in U.S. and Canada
$1.00 All Other Countries

Ballet flats on the cover of Vogue in 1949:
forecasting the decade of the gamine

they retained a prettiness required in an era where – as society had it – women were still primarily there to be looked at.

The ballerina as an ideal of female perfection helped with this – and developed over time. As choreographer George Balanchine put it, "ballet is woman". If, as we shall see, high heels objectified women as sex objects, the ballet flat fitted into another idea of what a woman should be: graceful, pretty and thin. Former dancers were the gamine movie stars of the 1950s: Audrey Hepburn, Leslie Caron, Cyd Charisse and, later, a young Brigitte Bardot. Ballet flats were part of their look – whether off duty in Picasso's studio in the case of Bardot, or on film in the case of Hepburn in 1953's *Roman Holiday*.

Several dance shoe companies already sold the designs. Along with New York's Capezio and London's Freed, there was Repetto in Paris. It is Repetto that is perhaps seen as *the* ballet flat brand now. Founded in 1947 by Rose Repetto, on the advice of her son who was a choreographer, the brand opened a boutique close to the Paris Opera and sold shoes to dancers. In 1956, they made the Cendrillon – French for Cinderella – at the request of 22-year-old Bardot. She wore the round-toed flats the same year in *And God Created Woman*, and the shoes were a girlish foil to the va-va-voom of the rest of her.

In recent years, Bardot has become more known for offensive and objectionable views around race, religion and sexuality – she has been fined five times in the French court for inciting racial hatred – and endorsing far-right candidate Marine Le Pen. Fashion, however, has not got the memo. Bardot has not yet been cancelled: images of her as a beautiful young woman remain fodder for newspapers, glossy magazines and social media. A fan account, @brigittebardotbb, has over 110K followers on Instagram, and her name has been lent to everything from an off-the-shoulder top to a hairstyle. The disconnect between her actions and the values of young people now may be striking, but there's little doubt the Bardot effect added glamour to the ballet flat.

*She wants to move: Leslie Caron shows off her barre
work in 1951 – a little girl's fantasy come to life*

In the 50s, the ballet flat was spotted on the Left Bank in Paris on
style plates like singer Françoise Hardy, in coffee bars in London and on
the Beat scene – almost always worn with black, to signify a difference
from the pastel-wearing mainstream aesthetic of the 50s. Beat poet
Diane di Prima took to this look. While studying at college in 1951, her
long hair and ballet slippers marked her out from her sweater-girl fellow
students. Instead, she "dressed like nothing they had ever seen on this
campus".[5] They were something of an artist signature too. Lee Krasner
and Georgia O'Keeffe wore them combined with paint-splattered shirts
and high concepts. Then there was white T-shirt woman, Jane Birkin.
She gave ballet flats a just-rolled-out-of-bed-on-Saturday insouciance,
one still analyzed on Instagram accounts and Tumblr pages today.

Fit for a princess

BY THE 80S, DANCEWEAR had enjoyed moments in smash-hit movies (*Fame, Flashdance, Footloose*), and on the dancefloor as part of disco. With the slogan "Danskins are not just for dancing", the leotard company grew: by 1978, it was earning $90 million annually.[6] *Fame* in 1981 – and Jane Fonda – helped make them, along with leg warmers, a fashionable way for middle America to signal they worked out; a proto-athleisure, if you will. An athletic body type, as toned as a racehorse, was the aspiration.

Ballet flats had a somewhat different trajectory. They were now worn by exactly the kind of women Di Prima took against – in Europe anyway. They were bourgeois. At Chanel, Karl Lagerfeld resurrected a Coco design in 1984, only a year after he became creative director. It was an early example of Lagerfeld's razor-sharp eye for a hit. The ballerina-type shoe, worn by icons of chic such as Inès de la Fressange, remains – along with the quilted handbag, the tweed jacket and, as we shall see, the Breton top – a hero item for the Parisienne. The book *How to Be Parisian*, published in 2014, included ballet flats in its list of essentials.

In the 80s, it's fair to say this chic didn't translate across the Channel. In Britain, the ballet flat was the preserve of the "Sloane". Writers Peter York and Ann Barr christened this new demographic – upper-class young people who congregated around London's Sloane Square – in *Harpers & Queen*. A *New York Times* article reported on them in 1976 as wearing an "English imitation of a classic French structured look" – hence those flats. In Sloane style, they were combined with padded headbands, pie-crust collars, longer skirts and big hair, making up a slightly dowdy look that sat halfway between SW1 and the country pile. Rather than a design for the new working women with disposable income, as Lagerfeld would perhaps have thought of it, the ballet flat here was part of a harking back to childhood. Upper-class young women would likely have attended dance lessons as children (Alexandra Shulman talks about them in her memoir), and wearing ballet shoes fitted into the Sloane's nostalgia for schooldays.

The ultimate Sloane, Princess Diana, sealed the connection between ballet flats and posh girls in the minds of the general public. Diana was hugely popular once her engagement to Charles was announced in 1981 – and often photographed. She wore ballet flats for royal engagements that didn't involve ballgowns, she wore them as a young mother, she wore them with – yes – pie-crust collars, and that big hair. She continued to wear them all her life, with French Sole a preferred brand – she bought 12 pairs there in 1993.

The Diana look has become hip in recent years. For a project featured in Sheila Heti's 2014 book *Women in Clothes*, fashion writer Thessaly La Force details how she dresses as characters for each month of the year. March calls for "Princess Di at a grunge concert", a look that includes black beanie, long pleated skirts and ballet flats.[7] The interest in Diana's style only increased with the release of season four of *The Crown* in 2020. It introduced her as a 19-year-old with an outfit consisting of chunky cardigan, dungarees and ballet flats.

Walking into ubiquity

THOUGH HER AESTHETIC could not be more different, Amy Winehouse was another woman in the public eye plagued by the paparazzi – and she shared Diana's love of the ballet flat. In the summer of 2007, Winehouse's exploits provided a seemingly endless stream of tabloid stories. The singer had a hit album to tour, a developing drug and alcohol addiction, and a new marriage to former video assistant Blake Fielder-Civil. On Friday 24 August,

Out and about: Amy Winehouse in 2007, wearing her
signature Freed ballet shoes and that other signature,
skinny jeans

the *Daily Mail* published images of the couple, bloody and bruised, after an alleged fight at the Sanderson Hotel. Winehouse has all her style signatures out of kilter. Her eyeliner flick smushed into her cheeks. Her beehive in disarray. Her skinny jeans ripped and misshapen. And her peachy-pink ballet shoes splattered with blood.

Winehouse knew the power of having a look, and ballet flats were part of that. The singer went for the extreme choice: actual ballet slippers by Freed of London, the kind she wore while studying at theatre school Sylvia Young. Intended for dance studios, their shelf life when worn on the streets of London was short. Speaking in 2016, her former stylist Naomi Parry said the duo would buy them "by the absolute bucketload ... I remember at the bottom of her wardrobe, she had mountains of greying ballet pumps ...We used to call it the Ballet Pump Graveyard."

While Winehouse was unique in her beehive and eyeliner, the singer was not alone in her take-up of the ballet flat in the 00s, even if others went for the more robust designs. Their resurgence began around 2000, when designers reassessed the shoe, with labels like Comme des Garçons and Issey Miyake collaborating with Repetto on versions of the Cendrillon. Sienna Miller wore ballet flats. So did a young Keira Knightley. It was another favourite of the paparazzi, however, who ensured young women made the ballet flat part of a uniform in this decade – one combined with skinny jeans, a blazer and bedhead hair.

Kate Moss began wearing Cendrillons in around 2003. Today, to say that Moss is a style icon is like saying the sky is blue. Arguably, the 00s was the decade in which she cemented the role. A model since the early 90s, Moss had a cute style as a teenager. It was slip dresses, it was Adidas Gazelles, slightly awkward jeans and hair that could have done with a bit more conditioner. By the time the new decade came around, Moss was a working twentysomething, a grown-up. Her day-to-day wardrobe, as they tend to do with age, had evolved to one of components: jeans, vests, silk scarves, ballet flats. In her quest to look more like a 1950s Bardot

– or at least more French – Moss had rescued them from the Sloane
cliché, brought them back from the fashion wilderness. I wouldn't have
dreamed of wearing a ballet flat in the 90s, but, worn by Moss, they
somehow looked fresh again. Here was a shoe that was, just like in the
40s, a way to look chic, low-key feminine but never too "done".

The new digital landscape – not to mention weekly magazines
like *Grazia*, which launched in 2005 – meant we saw more of off-duty
Moss in the 00s. We could study her day-to-day clothes and copy them
wholesale. I remember wearing my ballet flats with Baxter jeans from
Topshop and equally skinny T-shirts, and feeling like I had joined a
sort of Kate Moss club for the effortlessly cool. The bottom line of this
heroine worship was soon plain to see with her collection for Topshop
in 2007. It increased the store's profits by 10 per cent.

Moss had an impact on ballet flat sales too – in 2012, sales figures
were up by 76 per cent at Marks & Spencer and a huge 129 per cent
at John Lewis. This prompted *The Guardian* to declare the shoe "so
over". The very usefulness of the ballet flat – endorsed by Moss, now
something tens of thousands of women had cottoned on to – had
taken the shine off. Over 50 years, it had moved from arthouse to
something like average.

There were elitist implications here. Fashion insiders did not like
the hoi polloi wearing shoes that they had previously associated with
style royalty like Audrey Hepburn, or actual royalty like Diana. "I
remember walking into a store and seeing, for the first time, ballet
pumps stacked on the shelves like packs of chewing gum," fashion
editor Melanie Rickey says in the *Guardian* article. "I realized they had
become kit, rather than fashion." Ballet flats were now the preserve
of Oprah Winfrey's middle-American audience – the TV host
recommended foldable Tieks on her show in 2011.

Moss acolytes moved on to a new icon of aspirational
understatement: Phoebe Philo, then the designer at Céline. She
took a bow at the end of her show in 2010, wearing the Adidas

Stan Smith. Trainers quickly became the fashion-approved flat. Once reserved purely for exercise or travelling to work in, they were edging from something only worn by younger staff members towards standard office footwear in more and more industries as dress codes relaxed. In 2015 alone, eight million pairs of Stan Smiths were sold. By 2018, Isabel Spearman, former fashion adviser to Samantha Cameron, said it was now "acceptable to wear trainers not just to the office, but also in the office."

NEW SHOES

BUT EVEN NOW, when young women are likely to wear Air Max with a midi skirt, or (budget dependent) Balenciaga Triple S's with mom jeans, the ballet flat is far from invisible – it's still a useful go-to for women everywhere. Its place in our modern world was sealed in 2017, with a new software update on smartphones. PR executive Florie Hutchinson, annoyed by the red stiletto emoji as the default women's shoe option, started a campaign for flat shoes in the emoji-verse, nominating the ballet flat. "We need emoji that a majority of women can identify with," she told the *San Francisco Chronicle*. "And we need emoji that don't sexualize the female form." She succeeded in her quest. A blue ballet flat is now on your emoji keyboard.

Hutchinson lives in Palo Alto, a Californian city where tech companies rule. It makes sense she chose the ballet flat as her flat shoe default. Women working in the industry have adopted a twenty-first-century knitted version of the shoe, made by Rothy's, Everlane and Allbirds. They have a cult-like fanbase, despite being very far from cool. "The releases inspire as much fervour as a Yeezy shoe drop," wrote Hilary George-Parkin in *Vox*, "except the hypebeasts are women with office jobs who just want some cute flats they can commute in."

Rothy's estimate that they sold around two million pairs in 2019.

In her proposal for her emoji, Hutchinson wrote she chose the ballet flat because it was originally for any gender and that it is now "perennial, democratic, inclusionary and non-ageist". But to see a simple dichotomy between heels as objectifying and ballet flats as empowering is to misunderstand the nuances of shoe-based gender politics now. As one critique put it: "The ballet flat emoji is just as loaded as the high heel." As in the 40s, the ballet flat might not explicitly sexualize women, but it does conform to existing ideas of what femininity looks like: delicate, pretty, graceful. Even 70-odd years after it first became fashionable, it still performs the trick of bringing comfort, while keeping the wearer in that gendered lane.

Until very recently, the ballet flat was a conservative choice, then – one in contrast to the gender-neutral feel of a chunky pair of trainers. It's worn by women who wouldn't want to raise eyebrows. It's Pippa Middleton rather than *Killing Eve*'s Villanelle, Holly Willoughby over Rihanna. There's an innocence to it – or so Anna Delvey, the grifter that conned New York from 2013, hoped. She wore ballet flats to her trial in 2019, after her lawyer advised against the more glamorous and worldly-wise stiletto.

Gender stereotypes aren't the only issue, as emojis once again demonstrated at the end of 2019, with yet another update. Along with the ballet flat, there was now also a pair of pointe shoes. Like the ones I dreamed of as a 12-year-old, and the ones that appear in any Google image search, they are that peachy-pink colour; the one meant to camouflage with a dancer's leg, so when she goes en pointe, an illusion of skin colour is maintained. Of course, not all women's skin is this shade, and the assumption here divulges much about the ballet world. As illustrated in this chapter, from Vreeland to Hepburn to Moss, ballet flat icons are far from diverse either. The child's music box ballerina is mute but she still speaks volumes: the ideal remains a thin white woman in tutu and pointe shoes.

In ballet, this is finally starting to change. There are more dancers of colour, and stars like Misty Copeland and Francesca Hayward. But, until very recently, their shoes remained that peachy pink, meaning women like Copeland and Hayward would apply panstick to shoes before performances – a laborious process known as "pancaking". In 2019, Freed worked in collaboration with Ballet Black, the company that celebrates dancers of Black and Asian descent, to finally make shoes and tights in colours that more closely match a range of skin tones. "To walk in and see shoes in your own skin colour is a real

Their own shoes: Ballet Black dancers Cira Robinson,
Sayaka Ichikawa and Marie Astrid Mence celebrate
ballet shoes in different skin tones

change in the ballet world," Ballet Black's director Cassa Pancho told *The Guardian*, adding, "The message I've taken away is that people feel very 'seen' by it." The issue is still live outside of dance, in the non-inclusive labelling on the high street – where retailers like Marks & Spencer sell pale pink ballet flats described as "nude".

BALLET CLASS

BALLET REMAINS DISTINCTLY behind an increasingly politically engaged zeitgeist, then. Which is why it is surprising that the ballet flat – hardly a feminist object, as we have seen – is fashionable again. In 2019, the same publications that made Moss's flats into the shoe of the masses in the mid-00s announced its unlikely return. "The ballet flat is back and no, we're not kidding," wrote *Grazia*. "20 reasons to reconsider the ballet flat," said *Vogue*. This is a shoe that, like the ballerina on her 32nd fouetté in *Swan Lake*, has stamina.

The ballet flat is on the catwalk – for Chanel and Molly Goddard in 2017, Dior in 2019 – and worn by influencers, the kind of people who now have the reach that Kate Moss did in 2003. Leandra Medine, the founder of the *Man Repeller* blog, wore a pair of Mansur Gavriel ballet flats in February 2019, and they sold out. A £35 Marks & Spencer pair worn by fellow influencer Erica Davies did the same. Alexa Chung wore sparkly ones on her *Next in Fashion* Netflix show. Adwoa Aboah is a fan of Chanel styles. The body positivity online community has taken to dance too – something previously seen as only open to thin people. Lizzy Howell, a teenager who went viral on Instagram and now has more than 200,000 followers, danced at Eurovision in 2019.

The return of the ballet flat tallies with the return of ballet class – as a new strand of fitness for grown-ups who may or may not have been subjected to "good toes, naughty toes" as children. In 2014, I started doing ballet again – or a take on it. First as part of the adult classes at the English School of Ballet and now, more frequently, at my gym, as part of a Barre Concept class, where women line up around the edges of the room and perform imperceptible movements in what we hope is a vaguely balletic way. I'm part of a trend here, one that ex-French *Vogue* editor Carine Roitfeld is signed up to, as well as models like Gigi Hadid. As discussed, the appeal of ballet for those who work in fashion comes as no surprise – both are industries that, in general, idolize thinness when it comes to female bodies.

In her book *Trick Mirror*, writer Jia Tolentino confesses that she regularly spends $40 on a barre class. She says these classes feel worth the price because they come with an aim and aspiration: the ballet body, one of honed, athletic – and almost virtuous – thinness. "Conceptually, ballet is essential to the pitch," she writes, adding "an exercise method even nominally drawn from ballet has the subtle effect of giving regular women a sense of serious, artistic, professional purpose in their pursuit of their ideal body."[8] Indeed, I exercise a lot, but nothing else gives me the feeling of disciplined grace I get after a barre class. Thinking about it, the mood boost probably comes from the feeling that I am just a little bit more ballerina. The exercise is almost beside the point.

Tolentino dates the barre boom to 2010. Women have now been doing pliés in exercise studios for more than a decade. The return of the ballet flat is part of its trickle-down effect, an example of being more ballerina moving from the exercise regime to the wardrobe. If, as Balanchine said, ballet is woman, it's also fantasy – and it's a powerful one. I, along with all the other women in my barre class, will almost certainly never achieve the ballerina's perfect balance between grace and strength. But, just like every time we line up at the barre, every time we put on a pair of ballet flats some infinitesimal part of us lets us dream of doing a pirouette like Pavlova.

A return: after years in the wilderness, the ballet
flat is back of fashionable feet, like those of
model Adwoa Aboah

HOW TO WEAR THE BALLET FLAT NOW

Look to Lee Krasner and Audrey Hepburn, not Kate Moss.
Sorry Mossy, but your era is too close to ours. Instead, go for artist chic (cuffed jeans) like Krasner, or cigarette pants and polo necks like Hepburn. Eyeliner not optional.

Make the investment
The Repetto Cendrillon is not cheap, but it is classic. Available in countless variations and colours, this is the blue-chip ballet pump. It will last far longer – and wear better – than its cheaper imitations.

Say no to skinny jeans
The ballet pump 2.0 is not one for the skinny jean. Instead, women like Adwoa Aboah and Brittany Bathgate pair theirs with exaggerated frills, slinky midi skirts and slacker denim. The result is *très moderne*.

A white shirt + ballet flats = underrated combination
Make your shirt bright white and sculptural, like Diana Vreeland, and wear with ballet flats. Something about the proportions give this mix the kind of elegance we all aspire to, but usually don't have time for on an average Monday morning.

Dial down the dance
Crossbody cardigans, hair buns and – it goes without saying – tights and tutus are all to be avoided. The ballet pump has its roots in dance, but literal dressing does you no favours. You are not and never will be Margot Fonteyn.

NEED TO KNOW

- Ballet slippers were first worn by dancers in the eighteenth century, thanks to Marie Camargo. Taking a role previously only for men at the Paris Opera in 1726, she raised skirts to calf length, and removed the heels from the shoes previously worn by dancers.

- They went from studio to street in the 1940s, as a flat for a new demographic of working women. First appearing in Diana Vreeland's *Harper's Bazaar*, they were then adopted by designer Claire McCardell as shoes for models in her fashion show in 1944. Even McCardell was surprised by their popularity. "I meant them for the home or the country club, not the subway," she later said.

- First picked up by beatniks and bohemians, by the 80s the ballet pump was bourgeois and worn by Sloanes in the UK. Princess Diana cemented the general populace's association between ballet flats and posh girls. She wore them from the 80s until her death in 1997.

- Kate Moss resurrected the ballet flat, when she began to wear the Repetto Cendrillon in around 2003, with skinny jeans. It was a way – as it was in the 40s – to bring comfort together with femininity. Millions of young women signed up to the idea.

- The ballet pump now is such an every-shoe that it is also an emoji – since 2017. Worn by thousands as a pretty alternative to trainers, it is also fashionable again, and on the catwalk at Dior, Chanel and more.

Jean-Marc Gaucher
CEO, Repetto

Jean-Marc Gaucher wears a striped, open-necked
shirt and sits in a room with a chandelier. This
particularly French take on refinement is all very on-
brand for the CEO of Repetto, the dance shoe company
founded in Paris in 1947. Since the young actor Brigitte
Bardot asked the brand's founder Rose Repetto to make
her a street-ready ballerina, the Cendrillon – as the shoe
is known – has been much like Bardot herself:
a symbol of French style across the world.

Gaucher is uneasy about leaning on the Bardot connection – thanks
to the actor's more recent Islamophobic, racist and homophobic hate
speech. "I bought the company 21 years ago, and we never use her
name," he says. "In France, Bardot, when she was young, she was a
myth. Now, Bardot expresses some values which are not the values
of Repetto."

How important, by contrast, is dance? "It's everything," Gaucher
replies. "The values associated with dance are femininity, grace,
elegance, movement, freedom and dedication. If you look at the age
group from 22 to 28, when a woman arrives at this period in their life,
all this vocabulary matches with them." He says even as the consumer
gets older, these ideas remain enticing. They also – so the rhetoric
goes – come free with the purchase of a shoe. Gaucher uses me as an
example. "Perhaps you are more than 28," he suggests, with a smile,
"[but] in your head, you are not your age, you are still in this period of
your life."

Gaucher says the boom of the ballet flat was between 2005 and 2014 and, "after [that], the sneakers came". He has, however, noticed a new uptake recently and credits the latest generation of young women coming of age. "When she was a teenager, she was not trying to wear the same shoes as her mother [hence the trainers]," he says. "But now she becomes a young woman and wants to show more femininity than when she was 15."

In the ballet flat market, the Cendrillon (or "Cinderella" in English) is the connoisseur's choice, and expensive at around £180 a pair. The design is known for the low cut at the front to show toe cleavage – apparently requested by Bardot because "that was more sexy, she wanted to be more sexy at this age" – and its comfort. That's thanks to the shoes being constructed like ones for dance rather than those for the street. "When Bardot asked for Madame Repetto to make the shoe for her, she [Repetto] didn't know how to do shoes because they only did dance shoes," says Gaucher. "We make the first ballerina like we make dance shoes and today we still make the shoes the same way." Indeed, the brand have set up a special school to teach students the technique, with 380 graduates so far. The factory in the Dordogne produces up to 2,600 pairs every day.

Gaucher, a man who likes an analogy, comes up with a good one when I ask how he will continue to ensure that the ballet flat and Repetto stay relevant. "For example, if you live with someone for 40 years, every day is the same," he says. "After a few years you are a bit fed up with the situation. If he is not able to bring you new ideas, new things to do, one day it is finished. It's the same with a brand. We have to surprise the consumers all the time." Gaucher, to give another example, says just that afternoon he had a meeting about producing shoes using vegan leather. Ballet flats made without harming animals, but with oodles of comfort and grace? Sounds like a shoe fit for many modern Cinderellas.

THE HOODIE

He liked doughnuts. And girls. And the movie
Friday. He had dreams of being a pilot. He messed
around in school. He did odd jobs, like babysitting.
He liked Arizona watermelon juice. And weed.
And his stepmum. He did not like his teachers. Or
fights. He was looking forward to prom. He liked
music – Tupac and DMX. And hoodies. Trayvon
Martin liked hoodies. "It could be 100 degrees
outside and he would always have his hoodie on,"
his aunt said.

Seventeen-year-old Martin was shot and
killed by George Zimmerman in February 2012.
Zimmerman, a neighbourhood watch volunteer
in his Miami gated community, thought Martin
was an intruder. He was, in fact, visiting the
home of his father's fiancée. In the transcript of
Zimmerman's call to 911 to report Martin, the
older man describes the teenager as wearing "a
dark hoodie, like a grey hoodie".

"He would always have his hoodie on":
protesters raise a picture of Trayvon Martin
at a rally after his death in 2012

DIFFERENT WORLDS, DIFFERENT HOODIES?

IT WAS IN THIS FAVOURED ITEM that Martin died – Zimmerman shot the teenager as he was making his way back from the shop. He had bought some Skittles, and some Arizona watermelon juice.

After his death, both of these items became totems of resistance for those marching to protest this latest shooting of an unarmed Black boy in the US. Protesters carried signs with the brightly coloured logos of the confectionery. And, almost without fail, they wore hoodies: the Million Hoodie March, a hoodie-wearing demonstration in honour of Martin, took place a month after his death. Activists on social media posted images of themselves in hoodies, too. And basketball players wore them in solidarity, despite an NBA ban – LeBron James put a picture of himself and his teammates on Twitter in hoodies. Democratic Congressman and former Black Panther Bobby L Rush even brought them into the House of Representatives. "Racial profiling has to stop, Mr Speaker," he said, while wearing a grey hoodie. "Just because someone is a young Black male and wears a hoodie does not make them a hoodlum."

If the hoodie was worn to protest Martin's death, it was also seen as an explanation for it. "I think the hoodie is as much responsible for Trayvon Martin's death as George Zimmerman was," said controversial Fox News commentator Geraldo Rivera. "You have to recognize that this whole stylizing yourself as a gangster … Well, people are gonna perceive you as a menace." When Zimmerman was acquitted, Rivera couldn't resist an "I told you so" moment. "I was right about the hoodie, wasn't I?" he said. "Trayvon Martin would be alive today if he wasn't wearing thug wear, if he wasn't wearing that hoodie."

For some – like Zimmerman and Rivera – the hoodie is threatening. For others – like Martin, and thousands of young Black men in the US – it's a uniform, it's comfort and it's protection. Speaking on the phone to his girlfriend and aware that Zimmerman was watching him, Martin put the hood up. This yin and yang is the tension at the heart of the politics of the hoodie now. As writer Troy Patterson put it in the *New York Times* in 2016, "The lingering question of the hoodie is simply: Who enjoys the right to wear one without challenge?"

As a white, middle-class woman living in Britain, I have that privilege. I have worn a hoodie for the majority of the time I have written this book, a cheap Asos one that keeps me warm. The same hoodie has coached me through hangovers, it's come with me to the shop when I have run out of milk. It's been tied around my waist at festivals, I have taken it on holidays as a way to keep warm on planes. I reach for it when I go out dancing and don't want to worry about losing something more precious. I pick my cat up when I'm wearing it and don't care about the fur he sheds. A hoodie is for days where what I wear matters little, when all I want from my clothes is warmth, comfort and a certain level of anonymity.

This may be a point of view I share with Mark Zuckerberg. The founder and CEO of Facebook is another modern hoodie wearer, but one who – in contrast to Martin – wears his hoodie without challenge. The white, middle-class Zuckerberg is now estimated to be worth about $54 billion. Starting his career as a college student, he still makes clothing choices that speak of the dorm room. Zuckerberg's hoodies are wilfully anonymous, almost non-clothes. But they're such a trademark that even the notoriously publicity-shy CEO made a joke about them in 2014 – posting an image on Facebook of his closet with nine grey T-shirts and eight grey hoodies with the practically winking caption "First day back after paternity leave. What should I wear?"

Martin in a hoodie can be read as a threatening youth while for Zuckerberg, it's an eccentricity, a quirk. He's a disruptor, bringing the clothes of the weekend into the suits-and-ties world of business. Zuckerberg has been criticized for his hoodie – an analyst in 2012 called him "immature" for wearing one to the Facebook IPO, a formal, suity occasion – but it's largely thanks to him that in Silicon Valley, the hoodie is now appropriate office attire, the uniform of a new alpha male. Reporting on a 2013 Harvard Business School study, *the New Yorker* explained that, when it came to success in our modern era, "Deliberate nonconformity shows that you can handle some ridicule because you've got social capital to burn." Zuckerberg's hoodie might look like an oddly innocent, norm item of clothing, but on a billionaire who shaped the world we live in, there's no doubt it's a status symbol, up there with Victoria Beckham's Hermès Birkin. "I'm so successful," it whispers, "I don't need to make an effort."

"A SOFT COVERING FOR THE HEAD"

NEITHER ZUCKERBERG NOR MARTIN would likely have given much thought to the origins of their hoodies – or indeed how the hood has travelled with us through human history, how it is in our myths, our legends and our fairy tales. Depictions of Telesphorus, the Greek god who represented recovery from illness, show him with a hood up. The Grim Reaper, a figure of death in folklore, wore a hood from the sixteenth century.[1] There's Little Red Riding Hood, where the design detail is the eponymous character's protection for negotiating forests, not to mention grandmother-impersonating wolves. And the hood is even mentioned in Shakespeare – in *Henry VIII*, Queen Katherine opines "all hoods make not monks" when she is suspicious of a cardinal.[2]

The hood existed in reality too, of course. The word itself dates to the fourteenth century, and developed from "hod", meaning "a soft covering for the head". It was a layer of protection from cold, rain and danger. The dramatic impression created by wearing a hood – as seen with the Grim Reaper – can perhaps be dated back to the cowl, the cloak with hood worn by the monks Queen Katherine was referring to. They're documented in the writings of St Jerome and St Benedict. Here, hoods were both a ritualistic set of clothes to mark those in the orders out from the general public, and a practical solution to keeping monks warm in chilly monasteries.

The hood can be hateful, too. It is cruelly ironic to think that before young Black men were profiled for wearing of hoods, they were worn by, and synonymous with, the Ku Klux Klan. While the Klan itself dates back to the mid-nineteenth century, the use of the hood came about when, as Alison Kinney writes in her book *Hood*, "Hollywood took charge."[3] DW Griffith's 1915 film *Birth of a Nation*, based on a book that featured Klan members in hoods, put the images on the newly thrilling cinema screen. The Klan saw their moment. Ex-garter salesman and Klan member William J Simmons began selling hoods and robes, realizing the striking look could recruit new members. It worked: 100,000 new members signed up in 16 months. "Their force came from declaring membership in a safe, privileged identity that was anything but secret," says Kinney. "The hoods made Klan membership cool."[4]

If hoods have, by and large, a male history, they have also been associated with feminine modesty and discretion. In the eighteenth century, women wore a hooded travelling jacket called the Brunswick.[5] Queen Victoria herself, that paragon of respectability, was fond of wearing a hood while riding horses, and they became quite fashionable for women during the nineteenth century, sometimes trimmed with fur. Later, designer Claire McCardell, a keen skier, used hoods as part of her sportswear-infused collections in the 40s. A decade later,

Cristóbal Balenciaga – forever impacted by the ecclesiastical clothing he saw while growing up in a devout Catholic family in Spain's Basque country – used the hood to amp up the drama of his designs. It worked wonders for his opera-attending socialite clientele.

From the sideline to the cinema

THE HOODIE ITSELF – made of sweatshirt fleece, with a drawstring in its hood and a pouch-type pocket – predates Balenciaga. Knickerbocker Knitting Company was established in 1919 in Rochester, New York. Abraham and William Feinbloom first made knitted underwear. They then had the idea to focus on producing the kits for collegiate sports teams, the demographic who already had T-shirts as part of their kit. The University of Michigan was the first to take them up on the idea – and word soon spread on touchlines across the country. The brothers changed the name of their company in the 1930s – appropriately, to Champion.

Hoods on sweatshirts were an innovative solution to a sporting problem – they were added as a way to keep athletes warm while on the sidelines. Originally called the "side-line sweatshirt", they featured detachable hoods. An advert from the 40s for the Champion Knitted Line shows it quickly became a hero item for the brand. With a series of stick figures in various designs, the parade is led by a flagbearer in a hoodie.

The hoodie had history as an item of the elite male, long before Zuckerberg got hold of it. Champion sold these sweatshirts in college bookshops from the 30s onwards, as demand for athletic wear grew. A sweatshirt with your college's name on became a fashionable way

Putting the hoodie through its paces: Muhammad Ali –
or Cassius Clay – training on London's Mall in 1963

to fit in on campus. By the mid-60s, the look was bona fide. *Take Ivy*,
the 1965 cult Japanese book on Ivy League style, shows the fresh-faced
preppy students in colleges at play, and "side-line sweatshirts" on athletes
training for boating events at Dartmouth. While still an item for sport,
that would change as the Ivy look went off campus. The clothing that

advertised those years at college – especially ones that implied you were a college athlete – became weekend wear for young men to signal to other Ivy League graduates that they too were part of this elite club.

As you might imagine, the same innovation that worked for athletes on the sidelines made these hoodies popular with construction workers, those working in cold storage, tree surgeons – anyone who worked outside all year round. The US Military Academy also wore Champion hoodies. Through pure practicality, the hoodie simultaneously became a component of workwear, and a regular in the wardrobe of the blue-collar workforce.

Star power helped it make the jump from an item with purpose to an item for aesthetics. Enter Muhammad Ali. The boxer, known as Cassius Clay until 1964, was endlessly photographed. The hoodie – part of his workout gear – became a dramatic device. See Clay, walking with his trainers down London's Piccadilly in 1963, hood up, pulled around his face; or another shot of him the same year, clowning around in the back of a car; or training in the snow in 1972, with only a hoodie and trackpants to keep him warm. While his legions of fans could never claim to be the Greatest, wearing Ali's hoodie at least allowed them just a little bit of association.

Hollywood also played its part. Dustin Hoffman, playing a keen runner in 1976's *Marathon Man*, gets inadvertently involved in a Nazi plot. In a scene used in the poster and as part of the publicity material, he is seen pointing a gun, wearing a navy blue hoodie. While this cameo may now be a little obscure, another 1976 hoodie-in-Hollywood moment has been viewed over 2.4 million times on YouTube and turned into a GIF: that of Sylvester Stallone's Rocky Balboa running up the steps in Philadelphia, wearing a grey marl hoodie. The collegiate connection was fading. Boxers – real and fictional – gave the hoodie a touch of glamour but one centred around masculine strength and power. This idea chimed with the working-class men already wearing them.

Stick-up kids, graffiti artists, "thugs"

ITS PRACTICAL DESIGN SAW the hoodie make its first foray into hip-hop, then a burgeoning scene emerging in the Bronx and Brooklyn, around the same time Rocky ran up those steps. While the hoodie and hip-hop feel inseparable now, it was nowhere to be seen at first. The street gangs – or "families", as some members put it – at the very beginning of hip-hop wore denim jackets with the sleeves cut off, and the name of their crew painted on the back. Those unaffiliated to a specific family wore a take on preppy – Lois cords, straight jeans, loafers, Kangol hats and Cazal glasses with no lenses.

As hip-hop grew, in block parties and Bronx nightclubs like Disco Fever, it developed into what purists now call the Four Elements: DJ, rapper, graffiti artist and b-boy, or breakdancer. It was the last two groups who took up the hoodie as part of their look – it helped the graffiti artist conceal their identity when embarking on illicit tagging of subway cars, and ensured the breakdancer could spin more smoothly on that piece of vinyl thrown down in a park. Speaking to *Rolling Stone*, graffiti artist Eric "Deal" Felisbret said that hoodies initially had a nefarious association – they were worn by shadowy "stick-up kids" who might mug those in the crowd. Soon, however, the uptake of the hoodie by sectors of the hip-hop community – arguably still wearing the hoodie to conceal their identity, but without the dodgy intentions of the stick-up kids – meant it became a badge of an insider. "The people that wore them were all people who were sort of looked up to, in the context of the street," said Deal.

If the protection provided by the hoodie was appreciated, the theatre of it played well too. Other youth cultures liked this combination, they "found [it] suitable for the important adolescent

Up, up and away: the hoodie was standard pre-teen wear by the mid-80s – as demonstrated in Spielberg classic E.T.

work of taking up space and dramatizing the self," Troy Patterson writes. These groups included the "straight-edge" hardcore skater scene. Like the graffiti artists of hip-hop, they were also pursued by the police, for skating in public areas. The hoodie helped skaters conceal themselves from the cops, and it became key to their look. Cult band Gorilla Biscuits' first album in 1988 featured a gorilla in a Champion hoodie on the cover. BMX culture embraced the hoodie too – with Elliott's choice of a Little Red Riding Hood-worthy red hoodie for that famous scene in *E.T.* a sign that this look was already a familiar sight on streets by 1982. In the UK, casual culture on the terraces of football stadiums gave way to acid-house raves. The hoodie – the bigger the better – became a much-needed layer to wear over your smiley T-shirt for a lifestyle that involved dancing all night in fields. It was also, more ominously, part of a manhunt in the US: a sketch supposedly of the Unabomber terrorist was released in 1987, with the suspect pictured hoodie up.

Gives good face: Tupac Shakur in 1992 film, Juice. *His hood-up stance became fashionable*

In hip-hop, the hoodie had become a fashion statement. Its involvement from the early years brought priceless authenticity. Run-DMC, who initially wore checked blazers, had been given a makeover. They now wore black sweatshirts and hoodies – with gold chains, Kangol hats and, of course, their Adidas. It was a look designed to connect with fans. "Dressing this way lets them know 'he's just like me,'" Darryl McDaniels said at the time.[6] The Beastie Boys and LL Cool J followed suit. The latter's video for 1990's "Mama Said Knock You Out" sees the rapper circle back to the hoodie's boxing heritage – he's pictured in a ring, hood up, shadows playing on his face. A Tribe Called Quest added bright colours, and African-influenced patterns, to the mix.

As hip-hop moved from the sound of a block party to the story of real life as a young Black man on the streets of the US, the hoodie's place in the movement remained. When things turn dark in Tupac Shakur-starring 1992 film *Juice*, hoodies – worn with hoods up – have a starring role. The Wu-Tang Clan's first album, released in 1993, features faceless figures all wearing hoodies, an ominous image. And Dr Dre, Ice Cube and Snoop Dogg, the figureheads of gangsta rap – developing on the west coast from the mid-80s much to the moral panic of middle America – all wore hoodies.

By the end of the 90s, hip-hop had gone far beyond the five boroughs of New York where it began. It was on *Yo! MTV Raps* in suburban living rooms, on the stereos in the teenage bedrooms above, and in closets. "Our nation's clothes, our language, our standards for entertainment, our sexuality, and our role models are just a few items that have been affected by hip-hop's existence," Nelson George wrote in 1998.[7]

The hoodie was part of that. Halifu Osumare, hip-hop scholar and director of African American & African Studies at the University of California, Davis, says this commercialization of hip-hop, which coincided with the hysteria around gangsta rap, is when the mainstream's idea of hoodie-as-threat – there in Rivera's comments

Samuel Ross
Creative director, A-Cold-Wall*

Growing up part of a liberal, working-class family in
Wellingborough, near Northampton, England, the hoodie
was just what Samuel Ross and his friends wore, likely as
part of a Nike tracksuit, or under a parka. "The hood and
the epaulettes at the top of a coat, these were signifiers that
were part of a uniform that you opted into," says Ross. "That
was your culture, these were your people." It changed for him
when he got to his mid to late teens. "Being a person of colour,
growing up as a child in a country where you're a minority,
the first 12 to 15 years of your life is almost like an onion skin
unpeeling, as society reveals its true intentions regarding your
place within it," he says. As this process happened, "That
garment becomes a bit more significant."

Ross might sound like an academic, but he is actually the creative
director behind brand A-Cold-Wall*. With more than 720,000
followers on Instagram, stockists like Ssense and Selfridges, and a
revenue of $1.7 million between 2016 and 2017, the hoodie is central
to an aesthetic that refines sportswear with the help of Ross's high-
level thinking. Is it a big seller? "Huge," says Ross. "In [the] Asia-
Pacific [region], particularly. I was speaking to a friend about how
different cultures utilize different codes to show cultural awareness, to
go against the grain … semantics and semiotics are used to speak on
behalf of oneself without actually saying anything."

The designer believes it is this communicative power that makes
the hoodie an alpha garment – when it's worn by the likes of Mark
Zuckerberg, Elon Musk and Kanye West. "All those names are
billionaires, aren't they?" says Ross, getting into the stride of his

theory now. "There's a perceived understanding that one can go against the grain and probably expedite one's journey if one fast-track[s] around the system versus going through the system. The hoodie is a good representation of that."

Ross is now an expert in designing hoodies for the kind of customers who wants to subtly stand out from the crowd, but also display their impeccable design taste – A-Cold-Wall* has produced hoodies since the early days of the label in 2015. He says it is a pleasure to put his spin on such a design classic – "to augment the hoodie" – but there are rules. For example: "You can't have a rectangular pocket on the front of a hoodie. No one would buy it." Drawstrings at the neck are also avoided for a "cleaner" look, and the kangaroo pocket (the pouch at the front) is essential so the shape isn't too wide. "There are all these codes to it," says Ross, "things you start to learn when you start chiselling into the hoodie."

The hoodie is worn by all, but it is also, as Ross argues, an item for those outside of society – be they billionaires or those disenfranchised from the mainstream. "To speak simply, [the hoodie] will always represent someone who feels like they fit outside of the box regardless of what facet or tier of society or industry they are in," says Ross. This circles back to Ross as a teenager in Wellingborough. "You're almost in this bubble, and the normality was working class and was hoodie, especially in my area," he says. "When everyone is against the grain, it's the new normal isn't it?"

Leaving home to go to university, Ross left the hoodie behind – until recently, anyway. With an eye on his 29th birthday, the designer is reassessing the garment as part of his personal semiotics. "It comes with a sense of peace, comfort and acceptance that you almost don't fit into society to a certain degree, which is completely fine." Is wearing your hoodie about owning that idea? "To a certain degree, it really is," he says.

about Martin – began to take shape. A demographic of young Black men wearing hoodies was – society deemed – no longer simply a clothing choice. "The hoodie has become one of those cultural markers of the gangster outlaw," Osumare told CNN. "So now when people see a Black man with a hoodie in the street, it becomes an image of a potential thug or gangster."

HUGGING HOODIES

IF THE HOODIE'S POSITION in American culture focused on race and gender, the focus was on class and age in early 00s UK. Hoodies were a symbol of so-called ASBO culture, after the Anti-Social Behaviour Act was introduced in 2003 by then-prime minister Tony Blair. Anti-social behaviour orders targeted infractions including graffiti, noise pollution and the wearing of hoodies – with 40 per cent of them handed to 10–17-year-olds, often in deprived areas, by the end of 2005. The profiling of those wearing hoodies as criminals was blatant. As the late streetwear writer Gary Warnett said in a talk for SHOWstudio, it became "the uniform that frightens people, the shopkeeper's worst nightmare".

Quite literally. In 2005, shopping centre Bluewater banned hoodies, a move backed by Blair. Various other shopping centres and schools did the same, to keep undesirables out. In May of that year, teenager Dale Carroll was banned from wearing a hoodie for five years. The hoodie then become a proper noun – one to describe a city-dwelling working class young person up to no good. The example that the *Cambridge Dictionary* uses illustrates the profiling: "A female police officer is pushed down a flight of concrete stairs by one of the hoodies and the other policeman is hit with a crowbar in the face." If Blair's agenda with the ASBO was to appease respectable

*The London Riots, 2011: the hoodie was demonized, but was it
actually the clothing of a frightened young person?*

types, Conservative leader David Cameron saw an opportunity to gain
advantage over his rival. While he never actually uttered the words
"hug a hoodie", a speech in 2006 urged his colleagues, "the people in
suits", to stop seeing hoodies as "the uniform of a rebel army of young
gangsters" and instead show some understanding for people wearing the
clothing item. Endlessly derided, the speech didn't endear Cameron to

the people he was trying to win over. A year later, on a visit to a housing estate in Manchester, the leader of the opposition was photobombed by a "hoodie", making a gun sign in his direction.

Young people did defend their chosen item of clothing. Rapper Lady Sovereign released a song called "Hoodie", and launched a Save the Hoodie campaign in 2005. But, crucially, the way young people showed their disdain for disapproval was in the way that young people have shown disdain for centuries – they didn't listen. They kept wearing hoodies. They became part of a uniform in urban Britain, worn on the street, in schools, on dancefloors, and by grime acts like Dizzee Rascal and grime crew Roll Deep. A photograph of the group in 2010 shows seven out of 11 members in hoodies.

In the UK, hoodie hate culminated in the summer of 2011, at the London riots. Less than a year before Martin's death in Florida, protests began following the police shooting of Mark Duggan in Tottenham. Across five days, there was unrest across London, with shops burned and widespread looting. Over 2,000 people were arrested with 3,443 crimes committed. The item most likely to be worn by offenders? The hoodie. Often featured in news coverage of the riots, it was quickly cemented as shorthand for violence and misbehaviour.

In *The Guardian*, Kevin Braddock wrote how "a generation's default wardrobe choice was transformed into an instant criminal cloak for London's looting youth", and compared the media's portrayal of these young people to their counterparts across the channel in Parisian *banlieues*. Riots had taken place there in 2005 with hooded youngsters the offenders. Braddock reads the hoodie beyond the hoodlum. He looks at it as not only a way to hide from authority, but also a way to protect oneself, as Martin did when he put his hood up. The hoodie shuts the world out when it feels scary and inhospitable. Braddock writes of "kids in hiding, afraid of being seen, and at the same time embodying in their everyday uniform the furtive tunnel-vision that seems to define their bleak, introspective vision of the world outlook."

COMFORT FOR EVERYBODY, JUDGEMENT FOR SOME

AS THE HOODIE WAS DEMONIZED as the clothing of a young person up to no good, it was also – simultaneously – a status symbol for the elite once again. In 2012, then-creative director of Givenchy Riccardo Tisci, a self-confessed hip-hop obsessive, began to include hoodies in his collections. One with a picture of a Rottweiler became a cult item, despite its $565 price tag. By 2016, hot brand Vetements sold out of an $800 baggy hoodie. Some designers of colour, the ones finally granted a seat at the fashion industry table, have showcased the hoodie. African American designer Virgil Abloh's striped-sleeve hoodie for his Off-White label – a snip at around $500 – became a favourite for celebrities including Justin Bieber, Bella Hadid and rapper The Game. Abloh's former assistant Samuel Ross, the Black British designer of Caribbean descent, is behind A-Cold-Wall*. Ross uses them too. Hoodies are a cornerstone of a brand that Hypebeast described as merging "British working-class uniforms with elements of Savile Row tailoring". Demna Gvasalia, founder of Vetements, summed up the appeal of a hoodie for high fashion: "When you put [a hoodie] on, with the hood … the whole thing moves up. It gives you that attitude."

Whatever the price tag, the hoodie now functions as an essential for a generation that lives their life increasingly online and in their EarPods. Lou Stoppard, who curated *The Hoodie* exhibition in Rotterdam in 2019, describes it as "a tool for inventing one's own personal bubble". As we went into lockdown in the spring of 2020, the hoodie emerged as the perfect clothing item for a society in a collective anxiety attack, one that wanted to protect itself from the world, shut it out, and feel warm and cosy, while – as the internet

The hoodie goes high fashion: brands like Vetements put the everyday item on the catwalk

advised – staying the fuck home. We bought hoodies in droves: trend forecasters Lyst reported them as a top search term in March and April, everywhere from the UK to Australia. Net-a-Porter's sales of sweatshirts were up 106 per cent in the same period, with hoodies accounting for 49 per cent of those. While Champion is the original, Lyst's stats show it's now Nike that is the world's go-to hoodie brand – during lockdown, the sportswear giant received a boost in sales thanks to the garment.

Even before the pandemic, in an interview with the *Wall Street Journal*, Kanye West – with his usual prescience – named the hoodie "the most important piece of apparel of the last decade". He's right. The hoodie can now be read as a design classic, something that is rightly in the permanent collection of MoMA. But part of the power of this design comes from the fact it will always carry controversies too. To be a young Black man in a hoodie is still, as Halifu Osumare says, to be viewed as "an image of a potential thug or gangster".

For the cover of *Citizen*, Claudia Rankine's 2014 poem on race in the twenty-first century, the poet chose to highlight this – by using artist David Hammons's 1993 eerie work *In the Hood*. Here, the hood of a hoodie is ripped from the garment, without a person inside, and mounted on an art gallery wall. Made after 1991 footage of Rodney King being beaten by police officers prompted riots in LA, Rankine's revisiting of this image 20 years later is a stark reminder that problems remain. When George Floyd was suffocated by a police officer in May 2020, he was wearing a vest. But the item he wore in the image circulated by activists afterwards? A black hoodie. "A hoodie is worn by everybody: kids, white men, white women, Black men," Rankine said to *BuzzFeed* in 2015. "But it clings to the Black body as a sign of criminality like nothing else."

HOW TO WEAR THE HOODIE NOW

Hood up

This is how activists on social media celebrate Trayvon Martin's birthday on 5 February – making the hood-up selfie as a no-words-needed protest. Seventeen when he died, Martin would have been 26 in 2021.

Show your allegiance

Whether it's your alma mater, a love of a certain band or a cause you feel strongly about, the front of a hoodie can – like the T-shirt – provide a way to say something even on days where all you want is a boxset and paracetamol.

The original and still the best?

Champion's hoodies – call them sideline sweatshirts when speaking to those in-the-know – have cachet because they were the first brand to do them. The design with the little red "c" as a crest has design classic written all over it. Not literally, obviously.

Go XXL

For both comfort and aesthetics, an oversized hoodie is a winner. Vetements', produced in 2016, fell over wearers' hands, while hip-hop stars like Snoop Dogg are partial to going extra-large in the hoodie department. You'll certainly feel wrapped up.

Hone your own hoodie

This is the kind of item that gets better with age – really. Treasure your hoodie, wear it as a comforter, for sport, for your sofa, for everything. Over time it will become the kind of piece that gains a love-worn feel. People pay good money for that.

NEED TO KNOW

- The original hoodie dates to the 30s – and Knickerbocker Knitting Company, later known as Champion. It was designed for a specific purpose – a sweatshirt with a hood zipped on for athletes to keep warm while on the sidelines.

- The hood is found in Greek myths, in Shakespeare and in fairy tales. Monks wore them on cowls and the Grim Reaper had a hooded robe, when pictured from the sixteenth century. Hoods are sinister in other ways, too – as worn by the Ku Klux Klan, from the 1910s.

- The hoodie's association with hip-hop began with graffiti artists and breakdancers in the late 70s – groups that used it for protection and warmth respectively. By the mid-80s, it had moved from practicality to fashion statement, as worn by Run-DMC, LL Cool J and the Beastie Boys.

- The item was increasingly demonized from the 00s onwards – as a symbol of anti-social behaviour by working-class youth in the UK, and a threat in the US, typically when worn by young Black men. This culminated in Trayvon Martin's death in 2012. He was shot by George Zimmerman while wearing a hoodie.

- The hoodie gained a new role in society during the coronavirus pandemic. Sales of sweatshirts were up 106 per cent on Net-a-Porter in March and April 2020, with 49 per cent of sales coming from hoodies. Nike is the preferred brand – the sportswear giant experienced a spike in sales in 2020's first quarter due to hoodie sales.

THE BRETON

In May 2004, I went to St Mary's in the Scilly Isles. Remote and otherworldly, there was something enchanting about this slip of land. I felt as if on a raft floating in the sea, with nothing but water in every direction. Cycling around the island, there would be only fields as far as the eye could see and then, suddenly, a table with local produce and an honesty box. Sand dunes, seafood and wildflowers feature in my memory. And Breton tops. I bought a Saint James design from a sailor's shop on a dock – thick navy-blue cotton with safety yellow stripes. It was sold to me by a fisherman with an uncanny resemblance to Captain Birdseye thanks to the requisite beard, rosy cheeks and twinkle in his eye.

An image of undeniable appeal: Coco Chanel,
Gigot and the original Breton in 1930

From ship to Saint Tropez ... to simply everywhere

BACK IN LONDON, I WORE THAT Scilly Isles Breton for years. I'm a stripes aficionado, and it joined my skinny-rib T-shirts, pinstriped shirt and wide-striped tiered skirt. But it always stood out, even jumbled up in the washing basket or folded in a drawer with its striped companions. Despite its new city environment, the whoosh of the waves on the dock was there, the squawk of seagulls, whenever I put the Breton on.

This is not just me indulging in a nostalgic moment while getting dressed. The romance of seaside style is seductive. Traditional Breton brands like Normandy's Saint James and the appropriately named Petit Bateau trade on city dwellers' desire for that whisper of the beach even while squished on a rush-hour train. In fact, the spirit of adventure on the high seas hooked even the most urbane of style mavens – one Coco Chanel.

THE STRIDENT STANCE, THE WIDE-LEGGED TROUSERS, THE BOB AND THE BRETON TOP

CHANEL IS NOW SO UBIQUITOUS a fashion reference that she is almost a meme. A corner of Instagram is dedicated to her well-worn – in both senses – quotes. There's "I'm for style, fashion changes too quickly," or "A girl should be two things: classy and fabulous." But the designer has far deeper roots in your wardrobe. Forget the pearls, the suits and monochrome colour palette that make up the cartoon Coco. The Breton top – worn, as the name suggests, by sailors on the Brittany coast and also known as the *marinière* or the *tricot rayé* – has Chanel to thank for its fashionability. There's a famous photograph of the designer, taken in 1930. She wears a Breton top, hands in pockets, with her Great Dane, Gigot, at her feet. The picture was taken in the grounds of La Pausa, the villa on the French Riviera that Chanel built after buying the land a year earlier.

The Breton caught the designer's eye – as well it might – by the sea. Chanel was part of the Côte d'Azur set, the one later immortalized by F Scott Fitzgerald in *Tender Is the Night*. Amber Butchart, fashion historian and author of *Nautical Chic*, credits Gerald Murphy – friend of Fitzgerald, guest of Cole Porter, Chanel's acquaintance – with tipping the designer off. On a trip from his villa in Cap d'Antibes to Marseille in order to buy boat supplies, he returned with several *marinières* too. Murphy was photographed in a Breton in 1923 and he distributed them to his friends – including Fitzgerald. A sun-filled photograph from 1925 shows the writer in a Breton, his wife, Zelda, beside him, smiling.

It's unknown if Murphy gave Chanel a *marinière*, but when she did see the design she clearly recognized it as an item that worked for her vision of emancipated, carefree style. Originally a milliner, she began experimenting with clothing by making what she wanted to wear herself. Her designs were for women like her – ones with the independence of mind to spurn the corsets and frills of the Belle Époque and instead wear clothes with an elegant simplicity. The Breton's unpretentious shape and bold stripes chimed with this principle. Chanel biographer Justine Picardie describes the designer's adoption thus: "As was often the case in her career, she was quick to distil its essence, absorbing it into her own style, and selling it to customers eager for her clothes."[1]

All at sea: the Breton in its natural habitat, on French sailors in 1934

It should be said here that while Chanel is a giant figure in fashion – one who changed the history of women's clothes – her personal politics are less than chic. Investigative reporter Hal Vaughan revealed in 2011 that, later in life, Chanel was a Nazi intelligence officer, charged with recruiting new agents to the Third Reich. These revelations have not rocked Chanel's reputation, let alone the giant corporation that bears her name: even now, Chanel remains a byword for fashionable elegance.

Away from the haunts of fashionable high society that Chanel and her friends occupied in the 20s, the Breton represented something else entirely. For sailors, it meant hard graft at sea. Stripes had been worn on ships from the eighteenth century onwards – with Nelson supposedly sporting a striped sock. They became required uniform on tops worn by seamen (the lowest order on ships, those ordered about by officers) in northern France from 1858 onwards. The development has been linked to the idea that stripes make it easier for men to be spotted against the waves if they fell overboard. As might be expected of the navy, the number of stripes on a regulation *marinière* is precisely specified: 21 white stripes of 20mm each, against 21 blue ones. On the 1858 design, some of which were produced by Saint James, the width of the blue stripe is precisely 10mm on the body, with 15 stripes of the same width on each sleeve. It is rumoured that the number of stripes is designed to purposely match the number of Napoleon's victories against England.

Ne'er-do-wells, transgressors, dropouts and beatniks

STRIPES THEMSELVES HAVE A RICH backstory. Michel Pastoureau, author of stripes history *The Devil's Cloth*, even argues they have accompanied us through the development of civilization. He sees them in everything from the indentation of rakes on soil in primitive farming to the franking machines used for stamps. Stripes are, says Pastoureau, "a cultural mark, one that man stamps on his environment, inscribes on objects, imposes on other men … everywhere, the landscape bears the mark of human movement and activity in the form of stripes."[2]

Over time, the symbolism of wearing stripes has shifted drastically. They have long been – and are still – associated with prisoners or those interned, with striped clothing worn by those at Alcatraz, as well as at Auschwitz. In medieval times, they stood for transgression. Literature depicts sex workers and lepers in stripes to signify they weren't like the rest of society; they were ne'er-do-wells. As time went on, though, the stripe became fashionable. They were worn by young noblemen happy to survive the plague and don a garment that made a strong statement – one that aligned them with those ne'er-do-wells. Later, they were worn by Europe's elite. The stripe's affiliation with France, one that is still there in the Bretons we wear today, comes post-French Revolution, when the striped *tricolore* flag became the proud symbol of the new *république*. In the late eighteenth century, stripes were worn on tailcoats by the intelligentsia as a way of showing allegiance to the *tricolore*, and to show that the wearer was in modish solidarity with the lower classes, such as servants who had long worn stripes.

Skip forward 130-odd years to Chanel's era, then, and stripes were a pattern that was part of the language of fashion. The Breton was just their latest incarnation. By the 1930s, the top had become a favourite of bohemian young men. It was so ubiquitous, in fact, that it was singled out in a campaign of what might be termed proto-hipster hate. A 1934 article in *Adam*, a British men's magazine, featured a picture of a young man wearing a Breton and a beret, smoking a pipe. "Unfortunately, we have encountered more than one man dressed like this on the Riviera," it read. "We urgently ask our friends to see that all grotesque individuals of this type vanish immediately." Regrettably for the readers of *Adam*, the popularity of the Breton with a certain demographic only grew. It became the item of the outsider artist, the likes of Pablo Picasso and Salvador Dalí – men who refused to live, or dress, by the rules imposed in the 30s and 40s, when men of a certain class adhered to dress codes of suiting.

C'est chic, or something like it:
Iowan Jean Seberg shows off her Parisian
cool in her trademark Breton, 1965

A jersey T-shirt like this – one that was designed to be worn by a lowly sailor, no less – was the symbol that they had opted out.

Post-war, the Breton's bohemianism chimed with the nascent beatniks emerging from the scene on Paris's Left Bank. The 50s was perhaps the first decade when the rest of the world fell hard for the louche side of French style. The crush was fuelled by photographs of French teenagers dressed in ballet flats, Breton tops and skinny black trousers in Montmartre jazz clubs, smoking Gauloises and engaging in serious conversations about Sartre.

Jean Seberg – ironically an American born in Iowa – epitomized this idea in *À Bout de Souffle*. While her *New York Herald Tribune* T-shirt made its mark on the T-shirt's trajectory, Seberg's off-duty look in the film is also integral to its place in the style pantheon – the crop, the eyeliner, the Breton top. Choosing a Breton over a twinset and pearls might sound like mere personal choice these days, but in the 50s it was radical. This was a decade when femininity in fashion was heightened and idealized. Wearing Breton stripes marked you out – and when conforming was paramount, that could be a major faux pas.

THE STARS – IN STRIPES

MOVIE STARS IN THE US BEGAN to join the Breton gang. James Dean and Marlon Brando wore the striped shirts as a subtle nod to the fact that they might be household names, but they were also card-carrying members of the intellectual demi-monde. Like with white T-shirts, jeans and, as we shall see, the biker jacket, this was priceless endorsement. Images of these stars in Bretons would have spread the stripes far and wide – even after Dean's death. The actor, in an authentic (and aptly named) Saint James, was featured in a posthumous publication called *The Real James Dean* in 1955, beginning the link between Dean's brand of cool and the Breton for legions of fans. Cary Grant and Audrey Hepburn – playing Breton-wearing Americans in Paris in 1955's *To Catch a Thief* and 1957's *Funny Face*, respectively – boosted the T-shirt's profile further still.

Yves Saint Laurent, who later called his ready-to-wear line Rive Gauche (Left Bank) – put a Breton on the catwalk in 1962. As the 60s progressed, so did the Breton's place in the canon of counterculture clothing classics. Jackson Pollock wore one, and Warhol's Factory in New York loved them too – a red-and-white striped Breton apparently denoted your place in the core circle of the scene. From around 1963, the Breton was worn by both Andy Warhol and his muse Edie Sedgwick. Sedgwick took to wearing them with either black tights or just knickers, as she was pictured in Warhol's 1966 film *Kitchen*. The Breton is now so tied to the artist's identity that it was sold in the gift shop in his 2020 retrospective at Tate Modern.

Both Warhol and Sedgwick would likely have been seduced by the style of the ultimate 60s Breton-wearer: Brigitte Bardot. As discussed in the ballet flat chapter here, Bardot is more recently known for her far-right views. But the French film star made the Breton her own in the late 50s and early 60s, as part of what became dubbed the "sex kitten" look. Exhibited by Bardot to perfection in a photoshoot on the beach at Cannes in 1956, this was a quality so alluring that the French president Charles de Gaulle called Bardot "the French export as important as Renault cars". The Breton was ostensibly modest and unremarkable – positively tomboyish – before Bardot put it on. She gave it a smoulder that Warhol appreciated. He duly made an homage as only he could – completing a screen-print of Bardot in 1974.

The trickle-down influence of Warhol meant the Breton was a component of the Lower East Side uniform in the 1970s. It was worn by Patti Smith, Robert Mapplethorpe, Debbie Harry, Iggy Pop

A strong look: Andy Warhol at the Factory, working out in his signature Breton. Edie Sedgwick was no doubt close by

and Lou Reed. Bananarama made the Breton part of their playful androgyny in the 80s. The group wore the top tucked into men's 501s. Madonna sported a similar version in the video for "Papa Don't Preach" in 1986. And Jean-Michel Basquiat, painting a tribute to Picasso in 1984, depicted the Spanish artist wearing his beloved Breton.

If Kurt Cobain's penchant for the top underlined its place in the grungy, downtown creative milieu during the 90s, Jean Paul Gaultier, who had famously dismissed grunge, was the man who made the Breton high fashion once again – by adding a period-appropriate wink. A native Parisian, Gaultier took the visual clichés of France –

Getting into the groove: Madonna gives the Breton
her trademark sass – and a bit of midriff – in 1985

the beret, the trench coat, the Breton, even the Eiffel Tower –
and reinvigorated them with a heavy dose of irony.

The designer's own public image was central to this campaign.
Gaultier appeared in a hyper-kitsch Pierre et Gilles portrait in 1990
dressed in a Breton, holding a bunch of daisies, the Eiffel Tower in the
background, as if on a postcard. He later said, "I would very much
like to live in a world of the kind Pierre et Gilles see." Gaultier took his
ownership of the stripes further in 1995 when his perfume Le Male was
released. The bottle was a male torso wearing – *oui!* – a Breton T-shirt.

A CERTAIN
JE NE
SAIS QUOI

MOVE TO THE 00s, and the Breton's symbolism morphs once again.
The item of clothing once worn by outsiders is now a given. Alexa
Chung and Kate Moss – those dictionary definitions of contemporary
style icons – brought it to the mainstream. Since the mid-00s, they
have worn Bretons, often by Saint James, usually with an insouciant
eyeliner flick and skinny jeans; often to Glastonbury, sometimes at a
fashion show. Its legitimacy as a Gallic classic was ratified when actual
French women began to wear the top. Bretons became part of the
ingénue aesthetic of Clémence Poésy, Lou Doillon's low-key look and
the more rock'n'roll take by Emmanuelle Alt, editor-in-chief of French
Vogue. This was such a moment that *The Guardian*'s Hadley Freeman
wrote a column explaining, "Why everyone is wearing Breton tops".

That was in 2010, and Freeman put it down to the fact that
"everyone in the world became obsessed with how the staff at French

Vogue dress". While the French *Vogue* moment has passed now, the French girl has arrived as a key fashion muse. With tousled hair, Gauloises, eyeliner flick and, yes, a Breton, she is in a lineage. The French girl is a cipher – a blurry facsimile – of the beautiful young people of the Left Bank in the 50s. (The fact that she is always a girl and never a woman is a problematic side note.)

A lack of tangibility matters little, however. By 2017, an article for the website *Racked* called her "a billion-dollar myth" illustrating the article with a mademoiselle wearing – you guessed it – a Breton. There are now multiple guides to how to get the French girl look on the internet, 5.6 million posts tagged "frenchgirl" on Instagram (as well as the account French Girl Daily, hashtags #frenchgirlstyle, #frenchgirlvibes and even #frenchgirlhair), and several books (in English) designed to coax your inner French girl out. One features no less than five Breton tops on the cover. The trend has boosted stripe sales too. In 2016, Saint James had a turnover of £43 million, with 32 per cent of that coming from sales overseas. If you can't get hair like a French girl's or have her daily routine of coffee on the Left Bank, at least you can wear her top.

LA PARISIENNE AND FISHERMEN

LA PARISIENNE IS ANOTHER CHARACTER familiar to fashion's corner of digital culture. Almost as prevalent as the French girl, and just as likely to be wearing a Breton top, 3.1 million posts on Instagram have been tagged "parisienne", while #parisiennestyle and #parisiennegirl are popular too. Scroll through to find, as with the French girl, all the clichés and signposts Gaultier played with nearly 30 years ago – the croissant, the Eiffel Tower, coffee, Metro signs, the French flag and, yes, the Breton top. Their purpose? To anchor these images, and the women who post them, in Paris, the very centre of fashionability.

La Parisienne dates back to way before the selfie. She has long been what author Agnès Rocamora calls "a shorthand for fashionable femininity", arriving on the scene in the middle of the nineteenth century.[3] Paris was the capital of female fashion, and its women the poster girls of that fashion supremacy. Their Gallic influence is still powerful over 100 years later – although *la Parisienne* has evolved into #parisienne and been joined by her almost identical twin, the French girl. Influencers like Jeanne Damas, Caroline de Maigret and Anne-Laure Mais are some of the living, breathing examples, and their Instagram accounts are full of not-quite-attainable elements for others to aspire to: perfectly tousled hair, the time to stop at a brasserie even on a weekday afternoon, and the ability to apply just the right amount of make-up. About 80 per cent of the gags in the 2020 Netflix series *Emily in Paris* involved the inability of the brash American Lily Collins to reach Parisian heights of nonchalance.

As they are increasingly globalized, these French archetypes are now being questioned – partly because of a shift away from fantasy and towards the authentic. Real Parisian women, tired of being figments of fashion's imagination, are setting the record straight. A French website recently published a piece exposing the reality behind the myths concerning their female population. It included the confession that the choice of a pastry on a Saturday morning might be feeding a hangover rather than aacting as a photogenic treat.

Rocamora points out that #parisienne almost always, once again, means a white, thin woman – indeed, all of the women I have mentioned here fit that profile – who presumably, has a private income that allows her to drink coffee in Breton tops all day, and never go to work.[4] With the calling out of privilege more and more prevalent, this figure of aspiration may be making her *sortie*. Alice Pfeiffer, a French

Emmanuelle Alt: the editor-in-chief of French Vogue
*... annoyingly good at showcasing the intangible style
of her countrywomen*

writer based in Paris, has written *Je Ne Suis Pas Parisienne*, where
she argues that real Parisian women are a diverse and not always
well-dressed group. "Who is this woman that the whole world talks
about," Pfeiffer asks, "but that no resident of the city has ever met?"
That remains unclear, but she is indisputably part of the reason we
all wear Breton tops.

Even if the French girl's influence fades, the Breton's place in our
culture remains pretty solid. It fits into "looking French", but also
dovetails with another zeitgeist-y preoccupation: that of looking a
little like a fisherman. *Vogue* named the Aran knit – which originated
in fishing communities off the west coast of Ireland – as the jumper of

the season in 2015, and these days you are as likely to see fisherman beanies, Aran knits and yellow raincoats on twenty-somethings in Peckham as on the high seas. This look is now becoming mainstream. Searching the term "fisherman" brings up over 100 items on Asos, while basketball player Ovie Soko, one of *Love Island*'s most-loved contestants, made the fishing hat his trademark item in summer 2019.

As more and more of us move towards a WFH lifestyle that requires nothing more than a Wi-Fi connection and a flat white, it makes sense that clothes that signal outdoorsy jobs – Breton tops, as well as lumberjack shirts and even hi-vis jackets – are increasingly appealing. The magazine *1843* calls this "fauxstalgia" – a way for digital natives to reject the screen-based global anonymity of now, and express a yearning for a simpler life through what they wear.

Fisherman fauxstalgia has its in-the-know markers – that Saint James Breton, a Stutterheim raincoat – and places of interest. In London, the shop Arthur Beale, selling all manner of sailing paraphernalia, is a destination. But not everyone buying clothes here spends time on the high seas. For a section of the customer base, these sea-worthy clothes fulfil a different function. As renowned fashion writer Tony Glenville says, they come "with integrity, [they are] real clothes and not 'fashion' – even though it is."

Stripes for all

GOOGLE "BRETON TOP" and you'll be confronted with 76.6 million results. The tops are in John Lewis, Boden, Joules, at Monoprix if you want that holiday feeling when you're back at home, at JW Anderson if you want a directional take, they're a bargain at £10 from Superdry, and available for the super-rich too – €1,200 at the Christian Dior pop-up boutique on the current

Alasdair Flint
Owner, Arthur Beale

**Arthur Beale sits on a busy intersection in Covent Garden, as
it has for around 500 years. The shop started life as a place
to buy rope, rumoured to have been made from flax from
surrounding fields (fields!), and it expanded to encompass
all things nautical and adventure-related in the nineteenth
century, supplying both Shackleton and the first person to
scale the Matterhorn, Edward Whymper. The shop was named
Arthur Beale in 1901, when Beale, a former shop boy, took over.**

These days, it's a kind of watery oasis found in the middle of a city
of landlubbers, but it has become a shop adored by the expert sailor
and urbanite alike. Among the endless reels of rope, canvas bags and
nautical paraphernalia – such as an entire section called "blobby
things" (adhesives to you and me) – it's almost impossible to find out
when Arthur Beale started selling Breton tops, says Alasdair Flint,
owner of Arthur Beale since 2014. I talk to him in the office at the
top of the store, up a set of rickety stairs, past shoppers, including an
older couple in deep discussion with a staff member about rope and
an arty woman in a floor-length Judd Nelson-esque coat. Flint's not
the first of the shop's inhabitants I run into – that would be Tilman,
his six-month-old Parson Russell Terrier puppy who is in the store
for the day. Once Tilman is pacified – "let me find a bit of bone,"
sighs Flint – we sit down to discuss the shop, and where it fits into the
story of the Breton top.

Flint, with his chunky sweater and hair that looks windswept even
indoors, is like a sailor straight out of central casting. He says sailing
is his "main passion" and he's been to the Arctic several times.

He has been shopping at Arthur Beale since he was 21 and, while sale of the Breton pre-dates his ownership, it was he that reinstated a floor of clothing in the store. There, one can buy smocks, sweaters (like the one Flint is wearing) and Breton tops. Arthur Beale stock only Saint James, and only the ecru and marine, or marine and ecru (one has thicker ecru stripes, the other marine). "We're not interested in fashion, we're not interested in the new colour range. In fact, we hate it," says Flint. A hand-painted sign on the wall expresses their point of view. It advertises "beautiful but practical clothing to keep you warm on land and sea".

If the shop isn't interested in fashion, fashion is certainly interested in it. Fashion colleges send their students to visit and Anya Hindmarch and Paul Smith are fans. "Paul Smith thinks this is the best shop in London," says Flint. He's aware of the enticing halo of authenticity that comes with buying a Breton from a shop where items are purposeful. "I think people like buying stripy shirts [here] because it is a real boating shop. It's been here for 500 years," he says, when I ask why people choose his shop rather than the nearest branch of Uniqlo. "They like the idea of buying from a real place."

A certain amount of these customers are vital. "We don't get enough sailors through the door to afford a shop in Shaftesbury Avenue," says Flint, adding, "our ideal product is something that is sea-worthy, and you would be proud to wear on a ship, but also you could sell it to anyone." The day I visit, several fashionable types – one in an actual yellow plastic fisherman's mac – gather outside. The cheery sales assistant says they have at least one Breton enquiry a day.

As I depart the store, I notice the weather has turned to what can only be described as squally. It's as if Flint made a deal with the weather gods, negotiating darker clouds to encourage that Breton purchase. Not everyone is, as it were, on board with the weather, though. On the street, I spot Flint and an apprehensive Tilman, reluctant to go for lunchtime walkies. Perhaps he just needs his own Breton.

millionaire's playground, the Greek island of Mykonos.

A sign that the Breton has reached critical mass, though, is the fact that its most prominent contemporary wearer isn't a fisherman, and certainly is not French. Far from it. The Duchess of Cambridge is a woman so British you can buy a tea towel with her face on it at any London tourist shop. Much has been made of her collection of Bretons, worn from around 2014 for everything a royal life involves – from meet-and-greets in New Zealand to hanging out with Prince George at polo. Thanks to her, small British brand ME+EM are on the radar of the many Kate Middleton fans, who have all dutifully bought up the three styles of Breton that she reportedly owns. Even her sister-in-law Meghan Markle has taken to the top: she wore a Breton on a royal tour of Morocco in 2019.

Middleton's fondness for the Breton remains undimmed. A woman known for her literal dressing, she donned a dress resembling tennis whites for Wimbledon, and often matches the colour of her clothes to a country's flag on state tours. A Breton and sailor-style trousers were chosen to launch the King's Cup Regatta in May 2019. It was exactly the kind of meme-able look the internet responds to. Cosmopolitan.com's headline read: "Kate Middleton just wore the ultimate French girl outfit and we're obsessed."

If once, the Breton was the choice of the outsider, Middleton stands for the opposite: respectability and the establishment. Kate is a dyed-in-the-wool nice girl. She's jolly hockey sticks, middle England, *Daily Mail*-approved. A Breton for her is a jaunty, practical and slightly sporty choice, as it is for probably millions of women. She might wear designer labels for evening engagements, but like other mothers of three in Britain, a Breton is her day-to-day choice.

It's also the sartorial equivalent of comfort food. It semaphores a gold standard of chic, but its uncomplicated design ensures it is never intimidating. This meant it had exactly the right optics to project during 2020's lockdown. Both Anna Wintour and Middleton wore Bretons for video conferencing appearances – as, no doubt, did

*Appropriately maritime: the Duchess of
Cambridge at the King's Cup Regatta, 2019*

many other women working from home. According to Lyst, searches
for striped Breton tops increased 36 per cent in 24 hours after
Middleton's appearance on the BBC.

The Breton's continual regeneration is down to the fact that it has
now been a fashion item for close to 100 years. It is part of the style
scenery. My Scilly Isles top has long gone, and I am dubious about
the whole French girl thing, but the Breton's reassuring style status
still has its effect. I'm hankering after a Saint James again, to wear
with raw-edged jeans in the summer. I know I am one of many, but
I'm OK with that. Gerald Murphy, Chanel – and indeed Napoleon –
didn't know what they started.

HOW TO WEAR
THE BRETON NOW

Mix it with streetwear
Modern fashion is all about the high-low. Mixing ideas up, rather than sticking to an on-message look, works best. With streetwear now a part of the wider fashion conversation, a Breton with, say, a Supreme parka brings a fresh look, one that says, "I wear my fashion history lightly, but I know my stripes." Or something.

Pair a classic with classics
Forget the street style stars at fashion week. The more discreet worker bees of the fashion industry love a Breton and wear it with Japanese denim, brogues, a mac from Margaret Howell. Put with these pieces, the Breton is among its peers.

Think 50s French starlets with an update
Audrey Hepburn, a young Bardot, Leslie Caron ... these are the Breton icons. Update the look with a little from the Alexa Chung school of dressing. Keep the eyeliner flick, but team it with denim cut-offs and espadrilles. Combining It girls in an outfit gains bonus fashion points.

Buy the best
Sure, the Breton is everywhere, but the real French ones are not only the best quality – they're also a sign that you know your Breton. This will mark you out. To be really authentic and part of the Breton in-crowd, buy Saint James.

Avoid anything that says "smart–casual"
It makes sense that Kate Middleton has worked out a uniform around her Breton. However, if you are not Middleton, you have no need to pair it with skinny jeans, wedges or blazers. Think differently to update the look – a midi-skirt, a slip dress, pyjama trousers, these are all acceptable.

NEED TO KNOW

- The Breton was first worn by sailors in 1858. The rumour is that the number of stripes is designed to purposely match the number of Napoleon's victories against England.

- Coco Chanel popularized it, but she didn't discover the Breton for the fashion set. That distinction is Gerald Murphy's. The American socialite was the inspiration for Dick Diver in F Scott Fitzgerald's 1934 novel *Tender Is the Night*.

- The Breton was a favourite of the emerging teenager in France after the war. Photographs of these adolescents in Bretons, black slacks and ballet flats were pored over by their counterparts in the UK and the US. Their outfits were imitated, with the Breton becoming the badge of the outsider. The French girls of our current era are their descendants.

- The Breton has a distinguished roll call of wearers – including Pablo Picasso. The painter wore the top in many of his public appearances, ranging from a 1952 photograph by Robert Doisneau to a posthumous 1984 portrait by Jean-Michel Basquiat.

- The top has had catwalk moments over the years. Saint Laurent put it in a collection in 1962, and Jean Paul Gaultier, Balmain and Givenchy have followed suit.

- Kate Middleton arguably made the Breton go mainstream. Her go-to brand is ME+EM; she apparently has three versions of the top from the label. She has also worn Ralph Lauren and J Crew.

THE STILETTO

In my early 20s, I pooled all of my precious Christmas money and went to the January sales in Bond Street. I wanted one thing – a pair of stilettos, the shoes to instantly transform me into the polished creature I believed I needed to be to fit in where I desperately wanted to, at the top table of a fashion magazine. I found said stilettos in the bright and shiny world of Miu Miu. They were gunmetal grey and had the requisite spike heel. I tried them on and was just about able to totter about on the store's lush carpet. The walkability made me splurge, and I left the store with what I really wanted: a Carrie Bradshaw moment, complete with a shiny bag containing shoes – and my new glamorous future – on my arm. Inevitably, the reality was a little different from this fantasy. I wore these shoes precisely once, struggling through a commute and scuffing the heels on the ridges of the escalator on the Tube.

The 50s bombshell: Marilyn's stilettos, seen here in 1956, helped her become the sex symbol of an era

KNIVES, NEEDLES AND
FLOWER WOMEN

THE LESSON? These shoes were made for a life of cupcakes and cosmopolitans, not public transport and a low pain threshold. I can't remember the last time I wore high heels. Gone are the days – thankfully – when the ability to walk all day in stilettos was a required skill of any self-respecting fashion journalist. Now, sneakers and flats are far more likely to be seen on the front row. This tallies with what's found on women's feet more generally: a Mintel report from 2016 showed that more women bought trainers as opposed to heels – 37 per cent versus 33 per cent.

And yet stilettos remain a shorthand for glamorous femininity. Seduced by what historian Anne Hollander calls "an authoritative grace [that] can transcend all danger, inconvenience, and absurdity", women buy into this aspiration at a young age. It starts with that rite of passage moment so often replicated in movies – where a little girl, typically, tries on her mother's far-too-big high heels.

It makes sense that an item that so represents femininity was first popularized in the 50s – a decade that, as we have seen, was dedicated to manicured ideals of womanly perfection. While it's debated who designed the first stiletto, it was definitely a man. Salvatore Ferragamo, Roger Vivier and, to a lesser extent, André Perugia are all credited, with the invention dated between 1948 and 1954. Re-purposing technology developed for the airline industry, the ability to fuse a strong metal pin with a plastic heel meant a shoe could take the weight of its wearer on a tiny surface area, with pressure relieved from the arch of the foot.

Ferragamo began experimenting in the 20s, after studying anatomy and engineering. Marilyn Monroe wore Ferragamos in 1956's

Bus Stop, and they became a key part of the star's ur-sex appeal.
One of numerous Monroe myths goes that she cut a quarter of an
inch off one heel in order to achieve her legendary bottom-wiggling
walk. An exhibition of Monroe's heels at the Ferragamo Museum in
2012 debunked this – each pair of shoes had identical four-inch heels.
Even without the rumours, Monroe utilized the props of femininity to
bolster her own myth-making. "I don't know who invented high heels,
but all women owe him a lot," she famously cooed.

Although she had a role in popularizing jeans for women, Monroe
was the complete 50s bombshell in a pencil skirt and heels. Roger
Vivier worked at the other extreme of the decade's idea of femininity,
designing for Christian Dior and his demure "flower women", who wore
the New Look. Vivier's stilettos – called the *aiguille* (needle) – date to
around 1954. "They finish the silhouette with a stroke of a pencil," said
Vivier. While flower women are a thing of the past, the brand still makes
the *aiguille* today, more than 65 years later.

The fact that we call these shoes stilettos, as opposed to *aiguille*,
suggests that Italians, and Ferragamo, did it better. Meaning "small
knife" in Italian, *stiletto* was the name given to the daggers used by
assassins in Renaissance Italy.[1] The word became synonymous with
these new spiky heels by September 1953, when it was used by the
Daily Telegraph.[2] By the early 60s, as Maude Bass-Krueger writes in
Vogue, "the aspirational Hollywood veneer gave way to accessibility,
as [the stiletto] became the shoe of choice for most women." This
was despite the fact that stilettos were sometimes banned by venues –
including the Louvre[3] – for fear of heel marks on floors, and seen
as the cause of back and foot problems.[4] There might have also
been objections from the burgeoning feminist movement. If
practical shoes worn for the war effort had meant a new kind of
walk-anywhere freedom for women, stilettos put them back in
their place. They were, once again, objects to admire rather
than people on the move.

SKY-HIGH PLATFORMS, HEELS FOR MEN AND MORE

BY THIS POINT women's feet – and men's too – had been suffering for fashion for centuries. Depictions of Aphrodite show the goddess in high platform sandals and Greek sculpture dating to the sixth century BCE show women wearing similar shoes.[5] *Qabaqib* high platforms, worn by both men and women in the Ottoman Empire, were designed for bathhouses to avoid burning feet on hot stones. The chopine, an extreme platform up to a metre high, was worn by fashionable women in the fifteenth century.

Heels became popular in the 1590s. Around an inch in height, early examples were made from wood and covered with leather.[6] They may have evolved from the extremities of chopine, or come from further afield. Queen Elizabeth I wore heels – in an inventory of her wardrobe from 1595, an entry reads "a payre of spanyshe lether shoes with highe heels and arches". In Asia and Turkey, it was typical for male riders to wear high heels so they could stay securely mounted on their horses while riding or in battle. While this had been the practice for hundreds of years in this part of the world, it was brought to the West in the sixteenth century, when travellers from "the Orient" returned with books showcasing the clothes and shoes worn by people from these faraway lands – and sometimes the items themselves. With the rise of Shah Abbas the Great in the seventeenth century, culture from Persia – now Iran – was on trend. European male aristocrats began to wear heels like those of Persian horseman.

If they were symbols of masculinity at this point, women wore heels too – with varied responses from the patriarchal societies they lived in. In England in the fifteenth century, parliament passed a law to protect men against women seducing them with high-heeled shoes. Any such offender would be "punished with the penalties of witchcraft".[7] A fashion for a kind of androgynous look in France in the seventeenth century meant women were ridiculed for cutting their hair in a "mannish" style and wearing their shoes: in this case, high heels. In 1690s Russia, they were becoming part of a male idea of what women should wear. Peter the Great passed a law that women at his court were to wear high heels, wigs and make-up.[8]

Transformed from a riding shoe in Persia to a European fashion statement, the impracticality of these heels meant they were unsuitable for working people, setting an early association with the elite. "The heel expressed the status of the wearer as they were quite literally at a higher level than the hordes of common folk," writes fashion historian Jonathan Walford.[9] It's no coincidence that we still use the phrase "well-heeled" when referring to wealthy or upper-class people, while "down at heel" refers to someone down on their luck, or shabby and unkempt.

Heels were seen at the court of Louis XIV. The French monarch, who was 5'4",[10] insisted those in his inner circle wore red high-heeled shoes, making them a mark of aristocracy across Europe, and a sign of bullish masculinity, of pomp and power.[11] The 1701 portrait of the king by Hyacinthe Rigaud has red-heeled shoes front and centre. The fashion spread to the court of Charles II in England. He adopted his cousin Louis's footwear after visiting him in France.

As men's clothes became less flamboyant during the eighteenth century, heels became more clearly women's territory. Society began to see them as an example of women's frivolity that contrasted with men's natural seriousness (men who were considered too concerned with fashion were dubbed "red heels" in France). As such, they evolved to become both part of a male idea of what women should wear, and objects of threatening sexuality.

Heeled shoes disappeared from fashion for most of the first half of the nineteenth century. Slippers were the fashion – the kind worn by Jane Austen heroines in screen adaptations. Joséphine, Napoleon's wife, apparently had 300 pairs. But heels returned with the fashion for the crinoline, the wide skirt of the 1850s which, with hooped technology, swung around the ankle, showing the wearer's shoes.

Boots were the default choice, with a degree of height – around two and a half inches by the 1860s. In 1868, *Ladies Treasury* magazine declared that "High-heel boots are universal", despite concern from doctors around the health of the wearers.[12] The Pined Pinet arrived around the same time, a straight, slender heel that fitted into the mould of the stiletto.[13] High heels were now more explicitly part of male fantasies too: they were a prop used in pornography.[14]

Shoes became easier to manufacture in the early twentieth century – meaning they were affordable fashion items for more people. The real gamechanger came after the First World War. As hemlines began to rise, what women wore on their feet was in focus. "Shoes, far from reverting to their former state of conventional obscurity, even more than keep pace with the rest of the costume," wrote *Vogue* in 1921.[15]

The shoes in the 20s were far from stilettos and often came with a short stocky heel – the kind good for dancing. Their popularity – and visibility – meant they were still a cause for controversy, though. Thanks to the pornography connection, heels meant sex to the male establishment, and respectable women wearing them in such a brazen manner – with those shorter skirts, no less – undermined long-standing structures of propriety. Some called for the imprisonment of shoe manufacturers, arguing that these heels were detrimental to women's health. There was a subtext, however. "Legitimate claims that certain shoes were damaging to the body were blurred with the idea that they would also damage the virginal, obedient female soul," writes Summer Brennan in her book *High Heel*.[16]

Nevertheless, the shoe – and the women wearing them – persisted. High heels were becoming a way for women to signal a street-ready femininity, of literally putting your best foot forward. The rise of the stiletto in the early 50s is part of this trajectory.

*Put on your dancing shoes: the stocky-heeled shoe, as
seen at a Charleston competition in 1926*

A political act

IF BY THE 60S the stiletto was run-of-the-mill, it hit something of
a doldrum in the 70s thanks to the decade's new favourite shoe: the
platform. For the first time since the eighteenth century, high shoes were
worn by both men and women. David Bowie, Marc Bolan, George
Clinton and all of Kiss wore platforms. "Rather than feminizing these
male stars, the shoes were perceived as dandyish, hypermasculine and
conspicuously sexual," writes Brennan.[17] As such, they paid tribute to
the pomp of Louis XIV's shoes all those years before.

Some men had long worn stilettos and other types of heels, of course, and continue to do so. The shoes are a key component of drag. As RuPaul has said, "I'm six foot four – hello. And with hair, heels, and attitude … I'm through the mother-freakin' roof!" In this context, heels are about subversion, self-expression, pushing against gender norms and demanding attention.

Ru and his All Stars are in a lineage. Cross-dressing has always existed – Abbé de Choisy is a notable example from the seventeenth century, and molly houses in eighteenth century London saw men dressed in women's clothes.[18] Drag as an art form dates back to around the 1880s. Former slave William Dorsey Swann has been called the first drag queen – he threw drag balls in Washington, DC, around this time. Swann, and others on this scene, would have had to contend with the US's masquerade laws. Initially designed to prevent imposters using disguise to evade legislation such as taxes, and differing across states, these laws didn't specify wearing the clothes of the opposite sex as a crime, but they were co-opted by the police to prosecute gender nonconformity. The three-article rule came into LGBTQ+ culture in the 40s and 50s – a rule-of-thumb that meant a person could avoid trouble with the police if they were wearing three articles associated with their sex assigned at birth. For anyone assigned male at birth to wear a shoe like a stiletto was a risk, but one that many took.

Both Marsha P Johnson and Sylvia Rivera – who both self-identified as drag queens – wore heels, and did so at the protests that followed the Stonewall riots in 1969. LGBTQ+ activist and drag queen Flawless Sabrina was arrested dozens of times for what she was wearing – notably in Times Square while promoting the drag documentary *The Queen* in 1968. You could imagine that stilettos might well have been on her feet.

More than 50 years later, gender non-conforming people are still targeted for what they are wearing. Until 2011, a man

Shoes of resistance: Sylvia Rivera and Marsha P Johnson wearing heels on a rally for LGBTQ+ rights in 1973

"impersonating" a woman could still technically be arrested in New York state. It was still illegal for a Muslim man to wear women's clothes and shoes in Malaysia until 2014, when a court overturned the law describing it as "degrading, oppressive and inhuman". This ruling was reversed the following year, and it remains an offence in other countries, including Brunei, Oman and Kuwait. With this backstory, Jonathan Van Ness's high heels on the red carpet, Marc Jacobs in his platforms, and Yanis Marshall – in heels on prime-time vehicle *Britain's Got Talent* – are all the more important.

Sex, work and Essex

BACK IN THE 70S and in the heteronormative world, the stiletto was central to the sex-centric work of photographers and artists like Helmut Newton, Guy Bourdin, Allen Jones and David Bailey. Bailey made his – somewhat problematic – preferences clear: "I like high heels," he once said. "I know it's chauvinistic. It means girls can't run away from me."[19] So-called "fuck me" shoes date back to the 70s too. A 1974 David Bowie song "We Are the Dead" references "fuck-me pumps". Punks, meanwhile, liked the fetish connection. The black stiletto could be a perfect example of psychiatrist Robert Stoller's theory that "a fetish is a story masquerading as an object".[20] Worn by a dominatrix, it's a prop in a drama, one about a woman having power over a man – in a sexual context at least.

They featured in pornography from the nineteenth century but ever since Peter the Great – and probably before – women in high heels have been objects of desire, and part of male fantasies. Much is made of the posture that the shoes put women's bodies into. Academic Camille Paglia called it "a classic hominid posture of sexual invitation". In 2014, a study put a young woman outside a shop, asking men to answer a survey. When she wore flat shoes, 47 per cent of men agreed. In very high heels, this figure rose to 87 per cent.[21] The extreme of this association between shoes and sex comes back to that familiar accusation, also levelled at the miniskirt, that women are "asking" for rape by wearing such "sexy" items. A Conservative MP suggested this of high heels as recently as 2013.

In the 80s, the role of the stiletto in women's lives was in the boardroom rather than the bedroom. As fashion journalist Harriet Quick puts it, "career women" created "an armoury of shoes that were couched in the language of combat and ruthless competition – 'killer', 'weapon', 'dealbreakers' and 'game changers'."[22]

The spikiness of a stiletto – named after a dagger, of course – was a "don't mess with me" trope, worn with armour-like shoulder pads and a slash of blood-red lipstick.

The 80s saw the white stiletto become synonymous with a caricature in the UK. The so-called Essex girl became the butt of many jokes for her supposed dimness and her big hair, short dresses and white stilettos. These jokes revolved around young women from working-class backgrounds who now had more disposable income and the cheek to form their own aesthetic. Once, aristocrats were the only ones with the lifestyles to wear heels. The legacy of this hierarchy remains over 300 years later. Without the requisite breeding, Essex girls and their stilettos were accused of being vulgar. The fact that these young women were subjected to this ribbing and yet continued to dress how they pleased meant they could also be viewed as radical. Germaine Greer called the Essex girl "anarchy on stilts".

MAKING THE WALK A LITTLE MORE FUN

THE PLATFORM RETURNED in the 90s – this was when Naomi Campbell fell on Vivienne Westwood's catwalk, and the Spice Girls stomped about in Buffalo boots. But it was towards the end of the decade that stilettos and other high heels returned with a vengeance – and four style icons to boot.

Sex and the City was first broadcast on US TV in June 1998. Across six seasons, it became required viewing to follow the sexual adventures – and misadventures – of Carrie, Miranda, Charlotte and Samantha. The season finale had 10.6 million viewers,

*Manolos, Choos and Louboutins: designer shoes
were de rigueur for Carrie, Samantha and friends in*
Sex and the City

watching Carrie's fairytale ending in the arms of a somewhat flawed handsome prince in the shape of Mr Big.

As any regular viewer would know, the real love interest is, of course, shoes. They provide entire storylines – such as in "A Woman's Right to Shoes" where Carrie defends a lifestyle that prioritizes $485 heels to a friend who had chosen a more conventional path; "Ring a Ding Ding", where Carrie gets herself into financial trouble after spending $40,000 on shoes; or "What Goes Around Comes Around", where she's mugged for her Manolos.[23] And there are also footwear wows in every episode, from Carrie's Jimmy Choos to Charlotte's Prada stilettos.

The stiletto's role in *Sex and the City* subscribes to a particular type of "because you're worth it" commodity feminism popular around the millennium. The fact that women were buying designer stilettos for themselves was read as the ultimate in independence, emancipation and empowerment. Like lots of young women, I bought into the myth. The *Sex and the City* era coincided with my Miu Miu moment.

Sex and the City has dated – some of the dialogue and storylines around race, sexuality and the trans community are painful to watch – but it is part of the show's legacy that names including Manolo Blahnik and Jimmy Choo are recognized world over, and that heels became the status item of an era. A 2000 *Newsweek* article quotes a buyer from Neiman Marcus who says Blahnik's sales tripled thanks to the show. As Nancy MacDonell Smith wrote three years later: "The high heel has replaced the diamond bracelet and the fur coat as a symbol of luxury."[24]

RED SHOES, CATWALK TUMBLES

CHRISTIAN LOUBOUTIN WAS worn on *Sex and the City* too. Founded in 1992, the brand became famous for the shoes' trademark red soles – and Louboutin knew the value. He launched a legal battle to protect them from copycats, winning in 2018.

Any student of French monarchy would know he wasn't the first to realize the power of red when it comes to high heels – he owes a debt to Louis XIV. There's also the 1845 Hans Christian Andersen story *The Red Shoes*, in which a pair of irresistible red shoes take control of their wearer's feet, ending up with her feet being amputated. This story was adapted for the screen, in glorious Technicolor, by Powell and Pressburger in 1948, and it came after cinema's most famous pair of red shoes: the ones worn by Dorothy on the yellow brick road in 1939's *The Wizard of Oz*. Made for $15 by costume designer Adrian, one pair sold for £451,000 in 2000.[25] Dorothy's magic shoes are now fixed in our collective imagination. Despite the protests around gender stereotypes, the red stiletto emoji is a modern hieroglyphic for transformative glamour,

Some red shoes have sadder significance: one of thwarted female self-expression. In *The Thoughtful Dresser*, Linda Grant writes movingly about spotting a pair of red heels in a pile of shoes displayed at Auschwitz. "It reminded me that the victims were once people so light-hearted that they went into a shop and bought red, high-heeled footwear, the least sensible kind of shoe you can wear," she writes.[26] Mexican artist Elina Chauvet has used the red shoe in work that draws attention to the hundreds of women who have been murdered in Ciudad Juarez since the 90s. Her installation *Zapatos Rojos* has been touring for more than a decade. It puts any number of red shoes, mostly heeled, in public squares everywhere from Michigan to Mexico City as tribute to, as Summer Brennan writes, "the women who are no longer here to wear them."[27] Red high heels are a symbol for women's rights causes, too – they are a common sight at the annual Walk a Mile in Her Shoes events, which see men march in heels against domestic violence.

Extreme for everyday

THE IDEA OF IMPRACTICAL footwear as a sign of status – a triumph of beauty over the mundane – began long ago, but arguably reached its peak in the 00s. Louboutin's Extreme Ballerina Heels 2 are an exercise in fantasy: the upper of a ballet shoe with a heel so high that entertaining the idea of walking would be a fool's errand.[28] This point of view on high heels is one that Louboutin has consistently expressed. "I don't hate the idea of comfort," he told *The Independent* in 2012, "[but] I would rather someone say, 'Your shoes look passionate and sexy', than 'Your shoes look so comfortable.'" Women including Kate Moss, Rihanna and Victoria Beckham have signed up to this

Suffering for fashionable footwear: Daphne Guinness in Alexander McQueen's Armadillo heels

idea. Moss described Louboutin's black Pigalle stiletto as "my go-to shoe," in 2014.[29] Victoria Beckham wore sky-high Louboutin platforms to the royal wedding in 2011.

The catwalk also had a part to play in making extreme shoes happen. In 2008, *The Guardian* ran a news story about models falling on the catwalk at Milan fashion week due to perilously high heels. This was underlined by Alexander McQueen's Armadillo boot from his spring/summer 2010 collection, a kind of hoof design with a mega platform and high heel worn by Lady Gaga and Daphne Guinness.

The Guardian pointed out this trend wasn't limited to catwalk models and celebrities. "Our bestselling styles this season have been extreme. I don't think our customer believes in compromise," Olivia Richardson, head of fashion buying at department store Liberty, told journalist Charlie Porter. Favourites at Liberty included high platforms by Nicholas Kirkwood and the notorious Tributes by Saint Laurent. I remember trying some of these on at a sample sale and having problems standing up, let alone taking a step. "I don't think practicality comes into it," Richardson added. "It's more of an empowering assertion of your own femininity." As recently as 2017, this rhetoric was still being wheeled out. Writing in her book, *Free Women, Free Men*, Paglia declared the stiletto, "modern woman's most lethal social weapon".

Coming down to earth

IT'S IMPORTANT TO stress that, as with any fashion item, any woman should be able to wear stilettos if she so desires, without any judgment. But, at a time when we are reassessing the role fashion items can play in everyday sexism, and flats – from trainers to ballet pumps – dominate, perhaps that desire is fading somewhat. In recent years, there has been consistent pushback against dress codes that demand heels.

In a protest against the "no flats" rule at Cannes in 2018, actor Kristen Stewart took off her heels and walked the red carpet barefoot. This followed her speaking out in 2017, saying, "If you're not asking guys to wear heels and a dress, you cannot ask me either."

Women in corporate jobs are fighting a similar fight, albeit in less glamorous environs. In 2019, writer Yumi Ishikawa launched the #KuToo campaign (a play on the Japanese words for "shoes" and "pain", and inspired by the #MeToo movement) in Japan to try and ban high-heel dress codes at work. Nicola Thorp, a British receptionist, who was sent home from work in 2016 because she wasn't wearing high heels, as specified in her employer's dress code. Although over 150,000 people signed a petition against such sexist policies, the government refused to ban them as part of the Equality Act. Thorp described it as a "cop-out". Ishikawa hasn't fared much better. In response to her campaign, Japan Airlines decreed their stewards no longer had to wear heels and the Japanese Ministry of Health, Labour and Welfare has committed to "rais[ing] awareness". But, at the time of writing, no legislation has yet been passed.

Writing about the wider shift away from high heels in *The Times*, Harriet Walker compared them to thongs and push-up bras, "part of a pornified past that now feels strikingly out of step". A 2019 *Vogue* article was titled "How the 2010s Killed the High Heel". "I'm so glad we're moving away from this idea and becoming accepting of our bodies," Olivia Pudelko, designer of brand Westernaffair, told writer Kate Finnigan. "Instead of causing pain to ourselves we choose comfort, practicality and what we find appealing." The most consistent sign that high heels are out of favour is in sales. Lyst said there was a 25 per cent year-on-year decrease in sales of heels from 2019 to 2020.

The coronavirus lockdown provided another reason to ditch heels. Millions of office workers – who would previously have worn them to work – were WFH and, in all likelihood, no longer wearing any shoes at all. Consigned to the same category as jeans and bras, heels felt like the

Red carpet disruptor: Kristen Stewart removes Cannes'
regulation high heels in 2018. She has since worn
sneakers to award ceremonies

vestiges of a previous, less comfortable, life. Sales of Birkenstocks and New Balance doubled at retailer matchesfashion.com.

However, we should dismiss the seductive powers of this shoe at our peril. Talking about how she wanted women to feel when wearing her collection of heels – including Day-Glo stilettos – made for Rihanna's Fenty line in 2020, designer Amina Muaddi said, "I want to enhance their own confidence, beauty and femininity. I want them to feel ready to take on the world and overcome their fears." The future might be female, but it's complicated. The stiletto remains both a symbol of the patriarchy and also one of female empowerment in the twenty-first century.

HOW TO WEAR
THE STILETTO NOW

It sounds really boring, but make sure you can walk in them
There's nothing worse than going out for the day and limping along looking for a chemist. Find a heel height that works for you and your lifestyle. Budget for taxis? Go as high as you dare. More of a bus person? Aim a little lower.

Have a spin
Stilettos worn with an LBD might be a classic, but it's the equivalent of an overplayed song. Mix them with baggy stonewashed jeans or even an out-of-the-house version of trackpants. These pieces will give a refresh to these oh-so-ladylike shoes.

Colour is an interesting option
We think of the stiletto as the black patent number, but new brands have added a different colour palette. Something about bright neon-green pair of shoes feels just a bit more punk rock on Thursday morning, doesn't it?

Study stiletto icons
From Marilyn Monroe to – yes – Carrie Bradshaw, women with a penchant for glamour are worth perusing. For style tips, sure, but also just to marvel – like Tony Curtis in *Some Like It Hot* – at the ability to walk in high heels.

Experiment with lower heels
Brands are now taking walking into account with shoes that have a heel, but work for an eight-til-eight day. These can be chunky, or a modern take on the kitten heel. What they have in common is a lack of foot pain when you get home. Sounds appealing, no?

NEED TO KNOW

- The stiletto was first popularized in the 50s – a decade dedicated to manicured ideals of womanly perfection. Salvatore Ferragamo, Roger Vivier and, to a lesser extent, André Perugia are credited with making the first pair.

- Heels were first worn in the 1590s by the elite. Queen Elizabeth I, Louis XIV and Charles II were all fond of them. Some men continue to wear heels including stilettos. They have been part of drag culture for over 100 years.

- In the heteronormative world, high heels became women's domain, and a prop in men's objectification of women, from the seventeenth century. They came into their own after the First World War, when skirts were shortened. Stilettos since the 60s have been about sex – part of the fetish world for example – and power. Exhibit A: the career women of the 80s.

- *Sex and the City* ushered in a new age of the high heel – as the ultimate purchase for an emancipated single woman. Carrie's Manolos and Jimmy Choos were followed by extreme heels around 2008. "I don't think practicality comes into it," said a Liberty fashion buyer of the trend.

- Stilettos now are a Marmite item in a culture where feminism has taken root with a new generation of young women. Lyst revealed a 25 per cent year-on-year decrease in sales of heels from 2019 to 2020. But the desire still holds for some – see Amina Muaddi's sell-out collection of heels for Rihanna's Fenty line, released in 2020.

Shaobo Han and Henry Bae
Founders, Syro

A video call with Shaobo Han and Henry Bae, founders
of "femme footwear for everyone" brand Syro, is less a
conversation about now, and more a look into what could be.
Their brand began in 2016 and – at the time of writing – has
nearly 20k followers on Instagram, and fans including RuPaul
and Sam Smith. But New Yorker Han – the more talkative of
the two, sporting a very smart pale blue turtleneck – is keen
that the Syro story goes much further.

Asked for their goal, he says "it's really to normalize heel wearing
... [since starting the brand] they have become an integral part of
our wardrobe ... I want there to be a societal equivalent of that
[shift]." Their designs – plain to see behind the duo on shelves in their
Brooklyn studio – are about making that change.

Han and Bae pay tribute to gender non-conforming people who
wore heels before them. "I recognize the privilege that we can even
leave our house now," says Han. "It would have been an illegal act."
Syro's name, in fact, shows they're taking the long view. "It derives
from *anasyromenos*," says Bae, a slightly more serious presence in a
Black Flag T-shirt. "It was a term used to describe certain statues in
the Hellenistic period. There would be goddesses lifting their skirts and
there would be a penis. It was a positive symbol to ward off evil spirits.
When we came across that we were like 'wow, these kind of gender
fluidities have existed for centuries' but in modern society, it's become
very taboo."

The duo come up against this taboo every day when walking down
the street. "I think, as often as someone will ask me if I am Chinese

or where I am from, to the same degree people will say 'what are those?' or 'he's wearing heels'," says LA native Bae. Sometimes, these experiences can become violent. "There was an incident last year on the train for me, and for Henry I think a few times on the street," says Han. "And we recognize our own privilege by living in New York which is already such a liberal progressive bubble ... Safety is definitely the flip side of this whole freedom to express ourselves." Is wearing heels political? "Absolutely," says Han. "One of our mottos is to urge people to weaponize our fashion." "When I realized how awful it is that my femininity is stigmatized," says Bae "there was a part of me that was like 'I'm going to actively raise a middle finger – and part of that will be through wearing whatever I want to wear on the streets.'"

Syro is – intentionally – not just for celebrities. Their price points are around $230 (£180) a pair which, while not high street prices, allows more people to make an investment and buy into the brand. The styles also vary from the shiny-shiny platform Rancho, to the more everyday matt black Ami, both of which are bestsellers. "Normalizing is about wearing shoes every day," explains Han. "We want to create shoes you can wear to the office, for a casual stroll in the park, not just when you're going out to the bars."

Han, 29, and Bae, 30, first met online (on Myspace? "Facebook. We're not that old," says Han) and bonded over shared experiences of trying their mother's shoes on as children. "I didn't have the vocabulary to know why but I knew I could put my feet in my dad's loafers and that was fine, but these feet in my mother's high heels was absolutely not allowed," remembers Han. Asked about the appeal of the shoes, Bae responds, "Honestly I think that is so beyond my pay grade as a person. It's kind of like explaining to someone why I'm attracted to men, I don't know." Both agree that the act of putting on heels as adults is something that, as Han says, "feels correct. That's shared by a lot of our customers ... we hear a lot about when you put on heels it just clicks."

THE BIKER JACKET

In the mid-00s, while I was working at a fashion magazine, a friend and colleague bought an original punk biker jacket from eBay. When it arrived in the office, there was much admiration for the studs – it had so many that even picking it up was a workout. The real power, though, came when he put it on – thanks to the biker jacket's forever-cool quality, there was suddenly a frisson of curled-lip attitude, even in the after-lunch lull of a work day.

For more than 80 years, the biker jacket has seduced young men – and women – with the idea of the outlaw, zipping up in leathers, jumping on a motorbike and heading out on the open road. The Perfecto is thought to be the first, an invention of Schott that dates back to 1928 and is still made today. Founded on the Lower East Side in 1913 by brothers Irving and Jack Schott, the company first made raincoats for motorists.

*Brando, bike and biker: a legend pulls into town, or the
set of* The Wild One, *in 1953*

THE REBEL
YELL BEGINS

THE PERFECTO WAS designed for their motorbiking counterparts
– sold at a Long Island Harley-Davidson distributor for $5.50, it is the
first jacket to ever use a zip, after Irving came across the technology at
a clothing conference.[1] The version we know today, with diagonal zip
to protect the wearer from wind and help cover the neck, and cropped
shape with straps at the waist, arrived in 1940.[2]

It's been suggested that the first biker jackets were influenced by
jackets German pilots used in the First World War, the flying jackets
worn by Generals Patton and MacArthur in the Second World War,[3]
and even the black leather worn by the Gestapo.[4] But, in a sense, this is
all irrelevant. Primarily, jackets like the Perfecto worked as a practical
solution to keeping warm on a motorbike. That's why they were taken
up by a growing cohort of motorcycle enthusiasts.

The first motorbikes for commercial use were produced around the
turn of the century by companies including Triumph, Royal Enfield
and Harley-Davidson, which was founded in 1903. In the First World
War, Harley-Davidson produced 20,000 motorbikes for the US Army.
They were used to transport injured soldiers, but also in warfare –
with sidecars fitted with machine guns. This all helped with their
popularization post-war: the American Motorcyclist Association was
founded in 1924, and motorcycle clubs grew across America.

After the Second World War, biker culture struck a chord with
alienated veterans – typically working-class men – struggling with
civilian life. As Wino Willie Forkner, one of the leaders of motorcycle
club the Boozefighters, put it: "You go fight a goddamn war, and the
minute you get back and take off the uniform and put on Levi's and
leather jackets, they call you an asshole."[5] This was outerwear

in direct opposition to the respectable overcoats worn by those who did assimilate.

The threat to wider society from this contingent was crystallized in 1947, when 4,000 bikers from all over the US met in Hollister in California.[6] Across three days, the bikers made their presence known, with general revelry and more disruptive escapades – with one riding his bike into a bar and leaving it there.[7] While the incident has been exaggerated, up to 40 people were arrested, and the press were interested. A *San Francisco Chronicle* news report was followed a few weeks later by *Life* magazine, who published a picture – posed and taken after the incident – of an inebriated biker, with a 150-word caption.[8] By 1951, there was a short story. *The Cyclists' Raid*, by Frank Rooney, was published in *Harper's* magazine.

The facts of Hollister are somewhat beside the point. The media reaction built a myth, and introduced the biker-as-rebel character into US folklore. The pushback from bikers contributed too. Supposedly, after Hollister, the American Motorcyclist Association spoke out, saying that 99 per cent of bikers were "good, decent, law-abiding citizens", though they have since said they have no evidence of this statement. No matter. The title of the "one-percenter" was taken up by those involved in criminal motorcycle gangs, or those who just liked the bad-boy image. It's a badge of pride – literally – stitched to biker jackets to this day.

TOUGH, SOMETIMES ROUGH – AND READY

THE FICTIONALIZATION OF the Hollister riot was picked up by Hollywood. *The Wild One*, the biker film starring Marlon Brando wearing a Perfecto One Star, was released in 1953, with a plot broadly based on Rooney's story.[9] Billed as "the shock-studded adventures of this hot blood and his jazzed-up hooligans", it scandalized the establishment, but connected with the young and restless. Hunter S Thompson, in 1967, summed up its significance. "Instead of institutionalizing common knowledge, in the style of *Time*," he wrote, "it told a story that was only beginning to happen and which was inevitably influenced by the film. It gave the outlaws a … coherent reflection that only a very few had been able to find in a mirror."

After an initial downswing in sales when biker jackets were banned in schools, young people took to the item to convey their disdain for the conservatism of the era.[10] Like those other banned items, jeans and white T-shirts – and often worn with them – the biker jacket rejected the upwardly mobile personal style model, ie dressing to imitate the style of rich people. Instead, items that spoke of their purpose signalled status to bikers. "Finery was not their way – they preferred rough-and-ready, battered clothes which visually demonstrated their harsh experiences on the road," writes Ted Polhemus.[11]

Beside the seaside

THE SCANDAL OF *The Wild One* spread far and wide – and only added to the appeal of its look. This was particularly marked in the UK, where the film was banned until 1967. The ban did what bans tend to do – it only encouraged young people to emulate Brando and the bikers stateside.

The ton-up boys – and indeed girls – developed with the growth of motorcycles after the war and blossomed when petrol rationing ceased in 1950.[12] The name derives from "doing a ton" – exceeding 100 miles an hour on the motorbike.[13] They wore leathers, including trousers and biker boots, listened to rock'n'roll imports and gathered at roadside cafes. Biker jackets became, simultaneously, the prize item for these young people and, for the rest of society, a symbol of the danger they represented.[14] "Leather-clad" became the "hoodie-wearing" of its day; "a code word to signal delinquency", says Polhemus.[15]

The next generation of British biker jacket-wearing youth, the rockers, retained this lifestyle and look in the 1960s. More usually discussed alongside their supposed arch-rivals, the mods, the "feud" between these two groups began on Easter weekend in 1964, in Clacton-on-Sea. There were other clashes in seaside towns, including Margate and Brighton. Actual violence was minimal, but, as Dominic Sandbrook writes: "The newspapers were determined to present the fighting as though it had been a latter-day medieval battle."[16] The leather jacket was a symbol of the rockers' menace. "Youngsters Beat Up Town – 97 Leather Jacket Arrests" was the headline of the *Daily Express*.

In his 1972 book *Folk Devils and Moral Panics*, sociologist Stanley Cohen argues that the rockers – who venerated the heyday of rock'n'roll and the roadside cafe – were always painted as the losers. "The rockers were left out of the race: they were unfashionable and unglamorous just because they appeared to be more class-bound," he writes. Sandbrook echoes this. "Mods were both folk devils and fashionable trendsetters," he writes. "Rockers were just folk devils."[17]

Violence, revolution – and luxury

BEYOND THE ROCKERS, the biker jacket's fortunes in the 60s were mixed. It didn't fit into the peace and love aesthetic of the hippies, but it edged into catwalk fashion for the first time as part of Yves Saint Laurent's haute couture collection for Dior in 1960. The designer, just 24, was inspired by the *blouson noir* subculture in Paris. The collection included a coat with the same name, as well as biker-type styles.[18] It was all a bit much for the bourgeois world of couture: Saint Laurent was dismissed from Dior soon after this, but the designs were an early example of his game-changing talent for observing what people wore and turning it into high fashion. Fifteen years later, fashion writer Eugenia Sheppard credited him with "turn[ing the] black leather motorcycle jackets into high fashion, where they have been ever since".

Even with Saint Laurent's endorsement, the biker remained a threat when worn by the wrong type of young person. Richard Yates, that chronicler of mid-century American life, showcases this point of view in his novel *The Easter Parade*. Describing the arrival of the protagonist's nephew at a family gathering in the late 60s, he writes, "A hulking, squint-eyed youth came in, wearing a studded leather jacket and motorcycle boots, looking as if he meant harm to them all."[19]

Black leather was central to an emerging look pushing against the dominant white culture that the biker was part of. The Black Panther Party was founded in Oakland in 1966, by Bobby Seale and Huey P Newton, as an organization to fight racial injustice and poverty. In his 2016 book, *Power to the People*, Seale explains how they wanted a uniform, to mark out the Panthers as a force to recognize and to reckon with. "Leather jacket and blue shirt. I made it the uniform when we founded the party," he writes. Inspired by a blues song, "(What Did I Do to Be So) Black and Blue?", the idea was to visualize this feeling in clothing: "I'm saying the American community is all beat-up black-and-blue from over 200 years of racist discrimination ... Now, let's make this the uniform."

The Panthers' look has remained a touchstone of activism over the last 50 years, with Beyoncé's half-time show at the Super Bowl in 2016 paying tribute to it – complete with Black Power salutes. Activists from

In uniform: Black Panthers wearing their customary black leather, to protest the trial of The Panther 21 in 1969

the Black Lives Matter movement have used clothing to make powerful statements, like the Black Panthers before them. In June 2020, young BLM activists attended protests wearing graduation gowns.

Biker jackets – and riding motorbikes – were also becoming more popular with women in the 60s. Motorcycle journalist Anke-Eve Goldmann was apparently the first woman to wear a racing suit. She became the model for Rebecca in André Pieyre de Mandiargues's 1963 book *The Motorcycle*, which in turn inspired the 1968 Marianne Faithfull film, *The Girl on a Motorcycle*. Women wrapped up in leather became a peculiarly 60s idea of a sex symbol – see also Diana Rigg as Emma Peel in *The Avengers*.

The biker jacket wasn't done with havoc and violence, though. The Hell's Angels, formed in California in 1948, had spread by the early 60s to other states and as far away as New Zealand. The groups of men – women were characterized as "old ladies" rather than members of the club – on Harleys steaming through town centres, made them an object of fear. The look – long hair and biker jackets decorated with insignia – helped. The Angels were portrayed as the quintessential American outlaws and a menace to society. They were fictionalized in 1966 film *The Wild Angels*, and the subject of Hunter S Thompson's book *Hell's Angels: The Strange and Terrible Saga of the Outlaw Motorcycle Gangs* in 1967. This followed Thompson's *Nation* article two years before, tracking Angels' exploits including violence and gang rape.

The Grateful Dead had used the Angels as security, and manager Rock Scully recommended them for the Rolling Stones' Altamont concert in 1969, reportedly telling the band the Angels were "really some righteous dudes". The Angels were anything but righteous dudes at Altamont. They beat members of the crowd with pool cues and fists, and Alan Passaro, one of the security Angels, stabbed 18-year-old Black student Meredith Hunter. Hunter, along with three other people, died that night. Much has been made of Altamont as the anti-Woodstock, and the end of the hippy era. But the anti-Black racist violence is less talked about. As journalist Greil Marcus wrote later: "A young black man [was] murdered in the midst of a white crowd by white thugs as white men played their version of black music – it was too much to kiss off as a mere unpleasantness." Racism remains part of motorcycle culture. The Hell's Angels in the US still rarely admit people of colour into their chapters. Associations with white supremacy are part of their history, as well as that of other motorcycle clubs.

SID VICIOUS AND
TOM OF FINLAND – BUT
ALSO THE FONZ

PUNK IS THE HEADLINE reference when it comes to biker jackets
in the 70s. They were worn by luminaries including Sid Vicious,
The Clash's Paul Simonon, Debbie Harry and Patti Smith. Vicious
and his jacket were iconic, especially after the bassist – who wanted
to be buried in his – died in 1979. Studs and slogans were common,
the spikier and more controversial the better. Malcolm McLaren and
Vivienne Westwood were instrumental here too. The duo opened
their first shop, the 50s-inspired Let It Rock, at 430 Kings Road in
1971. Moving on from Teddy boy style, they went explicitly rocker,
with studded jackets, in 1972. The store was renamed Too Fast to
Live Too Young to Die, in honour of the epithet to
James Dean often written on the backs of bikers' jackets.

The biker jacket was also being – quite literally – drawn into gay
culture. The idea of leather as a homoerotic material dates back
to the post-war years, to the "leatherman" scene and subculture.
Tom of Finland, aka Touko Valio Laaksonen, added an extra
layer of fantasy. An artist known for his erotic images of masculine
archetypes ranging from sailors in uniform to cowboys with lassos
and bikers in biker jackets, his drawings became more widely known
in the late 70s. John Waters argues that biker icons like Kenneth
Anger, Joe Dallesandro, Jim Morrison and James Dean all owe
Laaksonen a debt. "None of them could have existed without Tom
of Finland's art coming first," the film-maker told the *New York Times*
in 2020. "He took the word 'butch' and turned it into a lifestyle.
No, a reason to live." The Tom of Finland effect could be seen in
everything from Robert Mapplethorpe's 1980 "Self Portrait" –

*All wrapped up: Debbie Harry out and about
with the biker jacket in the 70s*

"Butch, turned into a lifestyle": the biker as imagined by
Tom of Finland in "The Leather Brotherhood", 1980

with quiff, delicately balanced cigarette and biker jacket – to the
leatherman featured in the Village People's line-up.

By this point, the biker was established in Japan. Bill Haley's
"Rock Around the Clock" had been a hit when it was covered by
Chiemi Eri in 1955, and the *rokabirī* genre had been explored by
teenagers from the late 50s. The early 70s saw a revival, with bands
like Carol and the Cools sporting leather jackets and quiffs, and
performing rock'n'roll classics like Chuck Berry's "Johnny B Goode".
This is now an established subculture and exaggerated quiffs and
perfect biker jackets are still popular, as documented by Alvin Kean
Wong's 2019 photographs of rockabillies in Tokyo.

If Westwood and McLaren saw the biker jacket as radical,
Tom of Finland fetishized it, and kids in Japan used it to express
classic teenage malaise, wider culture in the US re-nosed it as part of
a cosy nostalgia fest. In 1974, *Happy Days*, the 50s-set sitcom, began.

Arthur Fonzarelli – the Fonz – was the textbook greaser complete with biker jacket. It may have been more than 20 years since *The Wild One*, but the Fonz was only allowed to wear that leather jacket while standing near his motorbike in the first season, for fear that he would look like a juvenile delinquent. This changed, of course, and the jacket is now so fused with the Fonz's national treasure brand of cool that it is in the Smithsonian collection. *Happy Days* paved the way for other nostalgia trips. *Grease*, set in 1958, was the second highest grossing movie of 1978. This relatability had its downsides – it arguably turned the symbol of rebellion into one of cliché. As streetwear critic Gary Warnett put it, the biker jacket "ceased to be menacing when Henry Winkler wore it in *Happy Days*".

THE BIKER TUNES IN – AND ROCKS OUT

IN HIS BOOK *Retromania*, Simon Reynolds talks about how all things 50s became a kind of cipher of cool in the 80s and 90s. "What the style now signified was ... style itself," he writes. "It had become classic, and *classy*."[20] Both Prince ("Kiss") and Michael Jackson ("Bad") played with this imagery. Arnold Schwarzenegger wears a biker in *Terminator 2*, with a Harley as accessory – a cyborg's idea of being inconspicuous in America – and Madonna for *True Blue* in 1986 subverts the Brando tradition of the biker jacket, by adding Monroe-worthy va-va-voom.

If it was overplayed, this idea did have a universality on its side. Reynolds points to George Michael in the video for 1987's "Faith". Michael's outfit – studded leather jacket, combined with Levi's jeans, cowboy boots and shades – helped him to break America, an example of a Brit taking American iconography and selling it back to them with aplomb.[21] Other acts attempting similar moves included Chesney Hawkes and Bros.

Aplomb wasn't lacking in heavy metal. Bands like Iron Maiden, Motörhead, Metallica, Judas Priest and Bon Jovi wore matching leather jackets – often with very impressive hair – on MTV and at spectacular live shows. With added studs, boxy shoulders and cropped silhouettes, they were key to a look designed to be as loud as the music. Judas Priest frontman Rob Halford was known to ride onto stage on a motorbike wearing leathers, including an impressively studded biker jacket complete with skull details and fringing.[22] If fans didn't go for the full look, they wore "battle jackets". Sleeveless vests in leather and denim, covered in the patches of favourite bands, they are a signature of heavy metal fan culture.

The biker jacket was worn by gay men with jeans and white T-shirts as part of the clone look of the 80s. Some gay women adopted them too. Writing in Emily Spivack's *Worn in New York*, photographer Catherine Opie says that, in the mid-80s, a 50s biker jacket "was the first piece of clothing that allowed me to identify as a leatherdyke." The subversion of bringing such a traditionally masculine object into a different context appealed: "I liked thinking, too, that the person who wore it before me was probably a straight white suburban man in his 50s and that wearing it was his way of looking tough, as if he rode a Harley."[23]

Leather was part of more mainstream ideas of sexy dressing for women. Designers like Claude Montana, Azzedine Alaïa and Thierry Mugler used leather, a material that had associations with masculine pastimes like motorbikes, but that – as the fetish scene had long observed – also clung to its wearer in a seductive way. At first, this look was seen as dangerous. Montana, whose career began in the 70s, was accused of taking inspiration from fascism because he combined black leather with huge shoulders. You could surmise that he also took inspiration from the leather clubs that he frequented. Whatever the genesis, the look suited the era. "It was the time of the masters and mistresses of the universe," said fashion critic Tim Blanks in 2015, "and Montana made clothes to dress these people like gods fallen to earth."

By the 90s, as catwalk designers explored leather to its logical conclusion, the allusions to fetish were made explicit. Gianni Versace's AW92 collection was entitled *Miss S&M* and shocked the fashion establishment with straps, corset detailing and lots of black leather, including a wide biker style worn by Linda Evangelista. The biker jacket here was the tame, almost conservative, end of a look that scandalized.

As the 90s went on, the mood wasn't to scandalize, it was to drop out. The biker jacket was out of favour in the grunge era. Too associated with heavy metal, acolytes of Kurt Cobain and friends were more likely to pull on a plaid shirt. In hip-hop, meanwhile, outerwear was more frequently a hoodie or varsity jacket. The biker jacket's wilderness years had begun.

The biker gets its groove back

I CAME OF AGE in the late 90s and early 00s, and I struggle to think of anyone I knew or admired who wore a biker jacket. In the world of Britpop, it was all about the parka, while when going out dancing, jackets didn't have much relevance to an evening when wearing a bikini top as an actual top seemed like a good idea.

This changed with a new wave of indie around 2002 with bands like The Libertines, The Strokes and Bloc Party. I remember seeing

The Libertines, a blur of guitars, sweat, spilled pints and leather jackets. Hedi Slimane brought the biker to the catwalk but not as the bombastic masculine tool it was for those 50s greasers or 80s heavy metallers. It was shrunken and part of a look that questioned the very idea that to be a man meant being physically strong, and into things like repairing motorbikes.

The 00s was perhaps the decade where the biker finally became as much part of women's wardrobes as men's. It was in Comme des Garçons' SS05 collection – which combined biker jackets with the tutus of ballerinas – Christopher Kane, and even Chanel. As Stephanie Kramer writes of the Comme des Garçons collection, the biker jacket is "a garment capable of imbuing the epitome of *soft* with the essence of *hard*".[24] Agyness Deyn, model of the moment, made this kind of contrast her own on the red carpet – often wearing a biker jacket with layers of tulle.

It wasn't just celebrities. Contrast dressing was a concept in most women's wardrobes at this point. With any reference just a Google image search away, the blending of styles felt apt for the iPhone era. Jenna Lyons, the woman who shrewdly brought great success to American retailer J Crew during this era with a contrast aesthetic, has described herself as "an equal-opportunities clothes wearer". She's fond of a biker, but might wear it with sequin trousers on the red carpet, with chiffon to a fashion show. Similar tricks could be performed with – say – a 50s frock with Air Max trainers or a man's shirt with a stiletto.

The biker jacket was moving into a position that is familiar to us today; as a versatile design with the kind of classic status that can't be disputed. Off-duty model style, at its height in the 10s, assisted the biker on this journey. Documented by street-style photographers outside fashion shows, young models were dressed in skinny jeans, black T-shirts, biker jackets and biker boots. The low-key nature of these clothes meant they were soon taken up by women who didn't walk runways for a living. In an article I wrote about the off-duty model trend, stylist Julia Sarr-Jamois said it was "quite an accessible look. People want to be the girl who can just get out of bed and pull on a jumper, whether it's the reality or not." This on-paper attainability may explain the proliferation of biker jackets far away from their open road origins. As Laura Craik, writing in *The Times* in 2013, asked of her school run: "Was I in the middle of a playground or a Hell's Angels convention? All around me they stood, MILFs in black biker jackets, glossy manes tumbling over leather shoulders, like pretty Axl Roses."

The biker jacket in the modern era is unusual in that it is part of a capsule wardrobe for women but – unlike the miniskirt, the stiletto or indeed the little black dress – it isn't about sex. It's a device to frame femininity with a contrasting toughness. That makes it that rare thing: an ageless fashion item for women. As influential retail maven Jane Shepherdson says to Craik: "Wearing a biker jacket is more a state of mind than anything as confining as an age limit. It can give an outfit an edge that no other jacket can."

Unlike most examples of clothes-related ageism, its actually men who run the risk of judgment when wearing a biker these days. Once seen as an item plump with testosterone (as worn by Marlon Brando, George Michael, even Pete Doherty), it now has the whiff of a midlife crisis, a last-ditch attempt to regain youth, up there with a tattoo or a sports car. The former presenters of *Top Gear*, Jeremy Clarkson, James May and Richard Hammond, are – whether they like it or not – the poster boys for this look. When Chris Evans took over the show in 2016, *Digital Spy* ran a feature on the trio's "history in ill-fitting leather jackets".

The "one-percenters" continue to give the biker a bad name. Violence between motorcycle clubs including the Hell's Angels, Mongols and Bandidos has increased in recent years. An incident in 2015 in Texas saw nine people dead and 18 injured, and smaller

*"Quite accessible": the off-duty model look, as worn by
Jourdan Dunn in 2015*

skirmishes are becoming more frequent. In this context, the biker jacket is still a way to specify your allegiances – it often comes covered in the slogans of the wearer's club, but can also signal far-right sympathies, including the twin lightning similar to the insignia of the Nazi SS.

Just an edge of edge

IF A BIKER BRAWL is one place where this jacket can be found today, it's far from the only one. You might see it while at the pub for Sunday lunch, or at a gig – it's as likely to be worn by a mother as her teenage daughter. Kim Kardashian and Kanye West wore matching bikers to their wedding in 2014 with the word "just" on the back of West's and "married" on Kardashian's. It's worn by Sharon Osbourne, Helen Mirren and Susan Sarandon as well as Selena Gomez, Gigi Hadid and Zoë Kravitz. Male musicians, including Bad Bunny, Playboi Carti, Pharrell Williams, Harry Styles and Jaden Smith, have taken to it too. So have customers of Mango, Hollister and Asos. Increasingly, for a generation concerned with sustainability and animal welfare, vegan leather is an alternative, with the environmental impact thought to be around a third of that of cow leather. Long used by designers like Stella McCartney, vegan leather is now used widely, with vegan biker jackets even available from Boohoo. It's estimated the vegan leather industry will be worth $89.6 billion by 2025.

Ultimately, the biker jacket now is perhaps the textbook example of how a giant of counterculture can be co-opted by the mainstream, but maintain a level of legitimacy. As Mick Farren writes in his book *The Black Leather Jacket*: "The biker jacket has become almost a paradox – an iconic item of clothing that symbolizes a separation from 'straight' culture, but which has been adopted universally."[25]

Alvin Kean Wong
Photographer

Halfway through his project photographing rockabillies in Tokyo, Alvin Kean Wong got a job that meant travelling briefly to neighbouring China. On his way back to Japan, his suitcase was searched, and the customs officer discovered a CD by premier rockabilly, "Johnny" Daigo Yamashita, whom Wong was photographing. "He asked every customs officer to come over," recalls Wong. "Everyone else at the airport thought I was caught with 15 kilos of heroin because there were, like, eight customs officers standing around me asking me questions about Johnny."

Yamashita is the leader of the rockabilly subculture in Japan, one that has existed in the country for 50 or 60 years, but is enjoying another renaissance. The musician – a pin-up bad boy with requisite quiff, snarl and leather jacket – has taken his band around the world, performing everywhere from Canada to the UK, appeared in a video for 5 Seconds of Summer and garnered over 30k followers on Instagram.

Wong remembers first encountering the rockabilly scene as a teenager travelling from Singapore. "We are a really conservative country," says the photographer. "So, for me, growing up is a struggle because I'm really weird and constantly I'm trying to seek out stuff, and the nearest stuff for excitement in culture and fashion is Hong Kong and Japan. When I first went to Japan, I was, like, 'These guys are so cool.'" Wong's weirdness worked out. Despite his father's initial scepticism, he now works for *Elle*, *Harper's Bazaar* and *i-D* magazine. He speaks to me from a sunny New York studio, surrounded by the ephemera of photography.

The young Wong was impressed by these rockabillies – most of whom could be found at Yoyogi Park in Shibuya, along with rockabilly women in bowling shirts and plaid shirts. But he says that wider Japanese culture shares the conservative attitudes he grew up with. "A lot of Japanese [people] are really locked down into expectations of what a person should do. 'You should get a job, you should make this much money, you should go to school'," he says. That means Yamashita and friends "stand out so much. If you see a normal Japanese guy walking in Shibuya, they are in a proper suit, nicely tailored, nice tie, impeccable shoes. You see Johnny – leather jacket, rockabilly hair, smoking a cigarette – the contrast is so huge."

The look is hugely important for rockabillies – with the biker jacket integral to the re-creation of the original 50s rock'n'roller still at the heart of the scene. "The Japanese rockabilly is the closest thing you get to Elvis," says Wong. "They are so obsessed with how they look. They won't put on a lot of weight because they don't want to look like a fat Elvis." Wong describes Yamashita's attention to detail: "The shoes have to be this way. If you go to the record shop with him, he will search out this old vinyl, that we probably don't know. The biker jacket is part of that."

Yamashita wants to make the scene something for everyone. He now dances, for example, in Yokohama rather than cool-centric Shibuya, and invites people to come and join in. The rockabillies will always appeal to each cohort of young people, says Wong. "Although [they] are a sore thumb in the society, I think a lot of Japanese have that romantic idea: 'It's really cool that I don't have to work in an office, I can be in a band, and during my free time I can build a car'," he muses. In fact, this free-spirit attitude is universally seductive: "Here we are looking at our stupid phones all day, looking at fake news ... we see guys like that living the life, playing in a band, travelling the world. They might not be millionaires, but they probably live a life better than most of ours."

HOW TO WEAR
THE BIKER JACKET NOW

No white T-shirt and jeans

Yes it's tempting, but, thanks to the Fonz, making like Marlon is too costume party now. Instead, contrast is your friend. The biker looks great, for example, over a floral slip dress. And go for trainers over biker boots.

Secondhand brings extra authenticity

An old punk biker jacket has more cachet than a high-street number. To get a good one, it's worth doing that eBay pro thing and setting up an alert. Lewis Leathers, Schott and – if you've got the dough – Hedi Slimane are your keywords. *Bonne chance*.

Know your references

Study everything from Linda Evangelista in Versace to Agyness Deyn on the red carpet and wedding day Kim and Kanye. Looking at what they wear with

their biker will help you bring your own take. Ballerina tulle, contoured makeup and fetish straps are optional.

It doesn't have to be animal leather

Vegan leather is worth investigating, as is other material. Christopher Kane has made biker jackets out of fluoro lace and snake-print chiffon, fabrics which add a playful feel. You might not have the designer budget, but take a look for a bit of inspo.

Get creative

The best biker jackets are the ones that communicate the thoughts and feelings of their wearer. This is an easy effect to achieve. Buy a basic version, and add studs, badges, patches and more. The battle jacket concept works beyond the metal scene, you know.

NEED TO KNOW

- The Schott Perfecto – which dates back to 1928 – is thought to be the first biker jacket. It was adopted by a growing cohort of motorcycle clubs in the US that developed when disillusioned veterans returned from the Second World War. An unruly biker convention in Hollister, California, in 1947 made the jackets a symbol of their wearers and therefore an object of fear.

- The 1953 film *The Wild One*, starring Marlon Brando in a Perfecto One Star jacket, fictionalized these events and made the biker go global. Taken up by teenagers in the States, the film also helped spread the jacket to the ton-up boys in the UK and the *rokabirī* scene in Japan.

- The 70s had the biker feature in spiky rebellion with punk, eroticism in the gay scene, and nostalgic fodder courtesy of *Happy Days*. The last example saw the item lose its edge somewhat – by the 80s, it was a universally understood symbol of classic cool rather than something to be scared of.

- After being in the doldrums in the 90s, the biker was put back on the radar of the young and the stylish by high fashion in the mid-00s. Interpretations ranged from Hedi Slimane's luxe indie boys to Comme des Garçons' pairing of the biker with a ballerina's tutu. The off-duty model look brought it to women everywhere.

- The jacket now is worn by brawling biker gangs, Sharon Osbourne, Jaden Smith, high-street shoppers and vegans. It remains – despite its popularity – an undeniable way to add just an edge of an edge to any look.

THE LBD

Most women will remember their first. Mine was PVC, it was from Miss Selfridge, it was sleeveless and reached the knee. Every time I put it on, I felt different. I was able to blend in, but be seen; be sophisticated, but – well, it was PVC – a bit rebellious too. Such is the power of the little black dress, or, indeed, the LBD. Long before in real life, big dick energy or Alexandria Ocasio-Cortez, the little black dress was known only by its initials. My PVC number has long gone, but I now have – surprisingly perhaps for someone who likes colour – an impressive count of LBDs in my possession. There are ones I wear for meetings – longer, with sleeves. Ones I wear for parties, including a vintage, flip-skirted design that I like to think is a bit Bianca Jagger at Studio 54. Ones I have kept for sentimental reasons – a corseted Marios Schwab number from my more extrovert days, and a velvet cocktail dress that belonged to my mum in the 80s.

"A sort of uniform": Chanel's Ford dress, as it appeared
in American Vogue in 1926

POWER – AND RELIABILITY

FINALLY, LIKE A lot of women, I have the tried-and-tested one, the if-all-else-fails one. In my case, this is a skater-skirt design from Monki. I've worn this dress for everything from a big day at work to a first date. It's both a source of comfort and a transformative item. Because, unlike any other item in this book, dresses – or certain dresses, anyway – have a kind of intangible magic. They can project the person you want to be, the person you are on a really good day. "Such dresses are not perfect forever, dating or wearing away over the years," writes Shahidha Bari in *Dressed: The Secret Life of Clothes*, "but while they last and while they fit, we feel in them as though we could tilt the world."[1]

The little black dress has its own set of superpowers. It is "an alliance of opposites," writes Didier Ludot, in his book dedicated to the item. "Between vice and virtue, the fantasy converges."[2] Initially, however, functionality was its USP. The story of the little black dress dates to October 1926, when Coco Chanel's seminal design was featured in American *Vogue*. To our eyes, the black crêpe de Chine, knee-length, long-sleeved dress is chic but quite everyday. But at the time, such simplicity was revolutionary, as was its colour. *Vogue* dubbed the design, model number 817, the "Ford dress", a nod to Henry Ford and his Model T car, but also his now infamous statement, that the car was "available in any colour ... so long as it's black." The magazine predicted – quite rightly, it turned out – that the dress, and ones like it, would "become sort of a uniform for all women of taste".

The Ford was not Chanel's first LBD: it is thought her first ever clothing design in 1913 may have been a black dress with a white collar,[3] and by 1919, her black dresses were described by British *Vogue* as a solution to "the general difficulty of living in Paris just now".[4]

Grief, reality and revelations

IT WAS A SIGNATURE item by the 1920s, if an alleged spat between Chanel and her rival Paul Poiret is anything to go by. Meeting by chance, Poiret – a famed colourist – is said to have asked the black-clad Chanel who she was mourning for. "For you, monsieur," she supposedly replied. Sadly for Poiret, Chanel was right: his era was over, and hers, with the LBD, was on the up.

Chanel was, as we know, a problematic character, but her gift for self-promotion, and her nous for assessing the precise tipping point for a style, allowed her to position herself as the visionary behind the LBD. In truth, although she helped to make it a symbol of a new kind of ready-for-anything chic, one we still buy into today, other designers including Jean Patou and Madame Premet made them too. And women had been wearing black dresses for decades – just not the kind of women who might buy a designer dress. With the exception of mourning, black was the colour of working-class young women – maids, shop girls and the like. Chanel used this as her schtick and a shock tactic to promote the little black dress, opining that "women should dress as plainly as their maids".[5]

This statement becomes complicated when you know Chanel herself came from humble beginnings. But the designer's background could go some way to explaining her attraction to black. Born in a poorhouse in 1883, the young Gabrielle was brought up in an orphanage by black-clad nuns after her mother died. Wearing black as a child to mourn her mother, it felt appropriate again in 1919, when her long-time lover, Boy Capel, was killed in a car accident.[6] "She later said that with his death she lost everything, but it could also be said that she gained a great deal," wrote veteran fashion journalist Colin McDowell. He sees Chanel's sadness – and her attraction to the black of mourning – as concurrent with that of other women around her who had lost lovers and husbands in the First World War. "Capel's death – as violent and saddening as death in the trenches – made a bridge between her and the rest of her sex."

Paris was recovering from the First World War, with over 600,000 French women made widows during the conflict.[7] If black – stark, sad, fundamental – expressed the mood, "little" had become fashionable by necessity, due to the economy drive around fabric during the war.[8] In *Black in Fashion*, Valerie Mendes points to an issue of the magazine *Queen* in 1917, which features four references to a "little dress" on just one page.

The colour of chic, but also rebellion

AFTER THE SPLASH OF the Ford in 1926, the LBD evolved into a device for wealthy women virtue-signalling in the Depression-hit 30s. "The emergence of the shop girl's simple black dress as a new and somewhat daring mode for leisured women was a striking sign of the spirit of the 1930s," wrote Anne Hollander. "Social conscience was expressed, as before and since, in clothes of upmost elegance."[9] Hollander also credits the black and white films, and characters in the lower orders, as part of the story. "It was these subdued and essential characters of the Hollywood legend, as much as the great sirens," she writes, "who furthered the romance of the little black dress."

By the 40s, LBDs were an everyday favourite. In 1944, when the world was at war, American *Vogue* declared, "Ten out of ten women have one, but ten out of ten want another because the little black dress leads the best-rounded life."[10] A little black dress was one of the items in the UK's wartime Utility Clothing Scheme. Edith Piaf wore a black dress – firstly because she had nothing else and then for its simplicity, as a way to focus all attention on her voice. On the flip side, Rita Hayworth wore one for a "wow" moment, as a vamp in 1946's *Gilda*. The tension between vice and virtue was coming into view.

Designers including Cristóbal Balenciaga, Elsa Schiaparelli and Christian Dior developed the luxury LBD in this era. Dior in particular was enamoured, coining the term "cocktail dress". The Diorama dress in his New Look collection used 29 yards of black crepe.[11] "A little black frock is essential to a woman's wardrobe," the designer later said. "I could write a book about black."[12] Yves Saint Laurent might have written his own tome. His designs for Dior (after Christian died in 1957) included the black trapeze dress (that proto-mini). His first ever item for his own label in 1961 was an LBD, and, as Hamish Bowles says, a see-through ostrich feather LBD from 1966 "freed the nipple way before it was a trending hashtag". Saint Laurent also has his own pithy quotes on black, including the slightly perplexing "a woman in a black dress is a pencil stroke".

It wasn't just women who could afford designer clothes who were wearing black. Black was embraced by Beats like Diane di Prima and her Parisian counterparts on the Left Bank. Author and academic Elizabeth Wilson sees this as part of a longer tradition: "Black had long been one signal of anti-bourgeois revolt," she wrote. "It was the combined influence of the dandies and the Romantics that made [it] a resonant statement of dissent."[13]

MOURNING, MASCULINITY AND MAIDS

THROUGHOUT ITS HISTORY, black clothing's rich symbolism has touched on everything from evil to death, status, bohemianism, piety and eroticism. It has been worn as the colour of mourning by Christians since the sixth century – and mourning Romans even wore black togas.[14] Its piety comes from clergymen and nuns, like the ones in Chanel's orphanage, who wore it. And there's the black worn by the Grim Reaper, and witches. These characters – so entrenched in Western society – perhaps explain the colour's connection to evil.

Techniques to dye fabric a "true" black were developed in around 1360 – and this made the colour luxurious. The fashionability of black has been credited to Philip the Good, Duke of Burgundy from 1419, who wore the colour to distinguish himself from his brightly coloured court, and also to mourn his father, who had been assassinated.[15]

Black spread through Europe to the Spanish aristocracy as a way to signal seriousness and prosperity, but also taste. In 1528, Count Baldassare Castiglione's *The Book of the Courtier* detailed life in Renaissance Italy, with the advice for aspiring couriers to wear black as a way to attain the "certain air of modest elegance" required for a position as both part of, and in service to, an aristocratic circle.

Hamlet wears black in ostentatious mourning for his father and, as the seventeenth century developed, the colour became a prestigious display of modesty for Puritans of means both in England and among settlers in the US. In Holland, as depicted in paintings by Rembrandt and Frans Hals, black was the choice of the upper classes. Speaking to *The Guardian*, art historian Betsy Wieseman said it was worn because it signified "sobriety and modesty. But at least as important was the fact that it was fashionable." When it comes to black, these qualities are often intertwined.

By the eighteenth century, black was worn across every strata of society. In around 1700, estate inventories show the colour was worn by 33 per cent of nobles and also 29 per cent of domestics.[16] The Romantic poets wore black as a way of expressing their melancholy. Lord Byron's 1814 poem "She Walks in Beauty" was said to be written after an encounter with his cousin's wife Anne Wilmot, whose mourning dress only served to enhance both her sadness and her looks. Dandies like Charles Baudelaire, Beau Brummell and Lord Lytton took to the drama of the colour.[17] While some berated what was seen as a miserable trend, thanks to black's association with death, Baudelaire "embraced and exaggerated" this element, according to Valerie Steele, director and chief curator of the Museum at the Fashion Institute of Technology in New York. No wonder, more than 150 years after his death, *The Conversation* call him "the godfather of goths".

If it was fashionable or edgy for men, women in black were either widows or, from the mid-nineteenth century, maids. The connection between servitude and black uniforms – still evidenced today by maids in posh hotels – dates to this era. Before this time, maids and their mistresses would each have worn their own clothes, but with brightly coloured prints and fabrics becoming cheaper in the Victorian era, an at-first-glance sartorial parity emerged. This meant, sometimes, the unthinkable happened – maid and mistress were mistaken for one another. Black came about to make sure – in no uncertain terms – everyone knew their place. *Cassell's Household Guide* for domestic service from the 1880s recommends "very dark or black French twill dresses" for housemaids.

In the States, fashionably dressed shop girls were forming a potential threat to the style hegemony of upper-class women in their finery. Restricting these interlopers to black – then seen as unbecoming and for mourning – put them in the background. Writing in the *San Francisco Call* in 1892, shop girl Rose de Haven dubbed black "undoubtably the worst thing one can wear in business", complaining that it was unflattering and made shop girls look like widows.

Women's mourning dress codes were in full effect in the UK by this point, amplified from 1861 when Queen Victoria adopted head-to-toe black to commemorate the death of her husband, Albert. Depending on their class, women adhered to certain social conventions, which meant wearing full mourning of only black for up to two years for a husband, then moving to half-mourning, when a touch of white and purple could be worn.[18] Upper-class women would have also added embellishment, including jet beading. These black-clad widows represented a significant sector of fashion's consumers.[19]

If they weren't in mourning, a young upper-class woman wearing a black dress could spell scandal; possibly because it messed with the social order, through the association with servants, but also because femininity was typically rendered in pastels, with bows and flounces (think of the girls in the Victorian decoupage paper stickers). The black dress was wilfully unpretty and plain. It was, therefore, the dress of the nonconformist, or the exceptional.

See Anna Karenina in Leo Tolstoy's 1878 novel, wearing black rather than the expected lilac of a young married woman at the ball where she first meets Vronsky, to great effect. Her dress is described as serving "only as a frame; she alone was noticeable". Unconventional Ellen Olenska also wears black at a coming-out ball in Edith Wharton's *The Age of Innocence*, as does the clever and independent Isabel Archer in Henry James's *The Portrait of a Lady*. Then there's "Madame X", the 1884 John Singer Sargent painting of socialite Madame Gautreau in a black dress. So shocking was the idea of an upper-class woman in something as plain as a black strapless dress – "aristocratically anti-bourgeois", as *The Guardian*'s art critic Jonathan Jones put it – that Sargent was forced to leave Paris and take refuge in England. The picture later inspired costume designer Jean Louis when creating his show-stopping dress for Rita Hayworth to wear in *Gilda*.

Hollander says Tolstoy uses the black dress to signal his heroine's "acute sexual readiness and tragic distinction". The fact that a black dress could stand for mourning but also sexuality meant it was the site of uneasy connections between style, seduction and grief. This tension reached boiling point during the First World War, when a widow risked societal disapproval if her mourning clothes weren't fashionable enough (she wasn't honouring the dead) or if they were too fashionable (she was a "fake widow").[20]

Chanel and other designers took this controversy and flipped the script only a few years later. "The seductive undertones of the widow's dress, which had been remarked on and vehemently criticized by the wartime press, became its main selling point," writes Maude Bass-Krueger in *French Fashion, Women & The First World War*.[21] In the 20s, a woman wearing black was more acceptable but still had a frisson of danger. It was associated with those who weren't willing to play by the rules, and brought an irresistible whisper of wild. No wonder it became so popular.

A NEW STANDARD

FAST-FORWARD TO THE 60s, and the little black dress was explicitly about glamour and seduction. The stars of European cinema wore black: Monica Vitti, Anita Ekberg, Jeanne Moreau and Catherine Deneuve. Audrey Hepburn playing Holly Golightly in 1961's *Breakfast at Tiffany's* brought an American take, albeit in a dress designed by a French aristocrat, Hubert de Givenchy. This design still epitomizes the modern ideal of the LBD, selling for $807,000 in 2006. It was – and is – sophisticated, elegant and sexy.

These weren't adjectives members of the youthquake were much concerned with – they wanted to look as young as they were, and had discovered colour. Although the brighter the better was the general rule, there were exceptions to this: Mary Quant had black dresses in her collections[22] and so did Barbara Hulanicki's Biba.[23] The portrait that The Supremes sent out to fans portrayed the girl group in matching black dresses, and the melancholy sight of Jackie Kennedy

*Three as the magic number: The Supremes' Mary Wilson,
Diana Ross and Florence Ballard in matching LBDs*

in black with a veil at her husband's funeral in 1963 is one of the most unforgettable images of the decade.[24]

Even with these moments, fashion was growing restless with the LBD: "It's so OBVIOUS," wrote the *Evening Standard* in 1963. "Aren't you bored with it too?"[25] It was so ubiquitous that Barbie had an LBD by 1964. The final death knell came in 1968 when Balenciaga retired. The thinking in fashion was that a certain ideal of the LBD – one of simplicity, elegance and structure – retired with him.

Youth culture revived the little black dress somewhat in the 70s, in ways Balenciaga would not have appreciated. Punk made LBDs out of rubber (not unlike the one I bought in Miss Selfridge) and rubbish bags, adding holes and safety pins. Disco brought a decadent, and slightly déshabillé, feel, with women like Paloma Picasso and Grace Jones wearing draped designs. It was the following decade, however, when style really went back to black.

A decade of dressing in black

THE LITTLE BLACK DRESS had it all in the 80s. Sexiness, present since Madame X and friends, became overt in a style that was generally short, tight and came to be known as "bodycon". Featured in the photographs of Helmut Newton, the video for Robert Palmer's "Addicted to Love" and worn by many a Prince protégé, the bodycon LBD was undoubtably about a male gaze but the female sexuality represented was powerful. As Nancy MacDonell Smith put it, this style was "not so much classic as dangerous".[26]

Then there was an experimental take on black, one associated with the artistic and the bohemian – or those with money, anyway.

Meet me at the Batcave:
goths' fun – and funereal – take on black in the 80s

Japanese brands including Rei Kawakubo's Comme des Garçons, Issey Miyake and Yohji Yamamoto began to show their collections in Paris in the early 80s, bringing a new abstract and sculptural approach to fashion. The amount of black in these collections was the headline story. In 1986, design critic Deyan Sudjic said that Kawakubo's clothes were "behind the wave of monochrome minimalism that has turned every fashionable gathering in London, New York, Paris and Tokyo into a solid all-black wall".[27] Yamamoto said the use of the colour was part of a wider Japanese culture and history. "The Samurai spirit is black," he said. "The Samurai must be able to throw his body into nothingness, the colour and image of which is black. But the farmers [also] like black or dark, dark indigo because ... the dye was good for the body, and kept insects away."[28]

Mendes argues that the ripple effect of this Japanese style meant black was part of the era's power dressing too. "This revolution offered a new direction for women's clothing," she writes, "The impact was enormous and far-reaching."[29] Black became the norm for the art crowd, the business crowd and the fashion crowd. But by the end of the decade, even Kawakubo was ready to move on. In 1988, in a proclamation worthy of *Zoolander*, she declared: "Red is black."

There was an alternative take on black in the 80s. The goth subculture, Baudelaire's godchildren, began to be spotted on the streets of the UK in the early part of the decade, and at club nights like London's Batcave and Slimelight. As goth royalty like Siouxsie Sioux and Patricia Morrison from The Sisters of Mercy showed, black was the chosen hue, inspired by gothic horror fiction, the dark cacophony of goth music, and kitschy references including *The Addams Family*. Goth black was spiky – leather and PVC – or romantic, with layers of lace, often worn with the kind of make-up that would scare Chanel out of her wits. Interestingly, this take on black remains. Black-clad goths are still a familiar sight on streets around the world, and indeed on subreddits.

Thinkers and
instant celebrities

IF TAKES ON BLACK were manifold in the 80s, the 90s saw seriousness and sexiness fight it out. For seriousness, designers like Donna Karan, Calvin Klein, Helmut Lang and Miuccia Prada made the black dress minimalist, with designs that worked for women's lives but also – in a very Prada way – commented on the everyday female experience. "To me, designing a little black dress is trying to express in a simple, banal object, a great complexity about women, aesthetics, and current times," said the always-erudite Miuccia.

A black Prada dress is unlikely to provoke jaws dropping on the floor – but some LBDs in the 90s did just that. Tom Ford's Gucci had the LBD as part of an aesthetic that could be described as sexy with a garnish of elegance. Princess Diana made an LBD central to the soap opera playing out in the royal family in 1994. Knowing that a documentary would air on television revealing that Prince Charles had been having an affair with Camilla Parker Bowles, Diana attended the Serpentine summer party the same night in a sexy, short, off-the-shoulder black dress by Christina Stambolian, one that framed Diana's athletic body and impressive bone structure just so. Images of her covered the front pages, with *The Sun*'s headline: "The Thrilla He Left to Woo Camilla". It was immediately dubbed "the revenge dress".

Also in 1994, a woman called Elizabeth Hurley wore what became "That Dress" to the premiere for her then-boyfriend Hugh Grant's film, *Four Weddings and a Funeral*. The Versace-loaned little black dress with safety pins along the sides and a to-the-thigh split catapulted Hurley – then an unknown – into the public eye, and she's remained there now for over 25 years. That Dress, meanwhile, is so famous that it has its own Wikipedia page.

*That Dress: Elizabeth Hurley enters the public eye,
thanks to a certain LBD, in 1994*

THE LBD
AS A FULL STOP

BY THE TIME THE 00S came around, the LBD was an item to endlessly reinvent. It was teeny-tiny on Victoria Beckham, ironically 50s on Lily Allen, corseted on a young Rihanna in the video for "Umbrella", rock'n'roll on Kate Moss who accessorized her cut-out Balenciaga LBD with a cigarette and a shaggy coat in 2002.

Neither Kate's Balenciaga nor That Dress – both of which thrilled the paparazzi – are likely to have had the same impact in the digital age. The thinking is that black dresses look "flat" on the screens of laptops and smartphones.

As social media became the most popular way to communicate, priorities shifted from making a first impression with those we were socializing with, to those who we are pals with online, and that meant colour ruled. "Patterns, print and colour is the easiest way to get noticed, receive likes and, sadly, validation," designer Catherine Quin, who launched an all-black collection in 2014, told the *Financial Times*.

Quin and many others were no doubt heartened, then, when the little black dress began to make its comeback in the last few years. This is partly due to technology. Newer OLED screens are able to render black better, due to better pixel densities, so an LBD stands out even if you're not IRL. This has seen an impact on sales: trend forecasting agency Edited noticed an uplift in the sales of LBDs from the start of 2017 to the following year, and the number of black dresses available on Zara's website from 2014 to 2017 increased by 145 per cent. Women continue to use the LBD as a jaw-dropping device, too. Adele, in her first Instagram post of 2020, revealed dramatic weight loss with a selfie of her wearing an LBD. Lyst reported that the dress sold out within hours, with the search for "black dress" up 67 per cent in the 24 hours after.

Once a way to put women in the background, the LBD is now a cliché of sexy dressing. An entry on *Urban Dictionary* from 2006 describes it as "for the sole purpose of seducing men". The connection was still there in 2018, when the dress code for "gentlemen's club" the Presidents Club was revealed, with young women working there required to wear short, tight black dresses with transparent side panels. While the club has now closed down, a clothing range using the same name was founded in 2020. The first item for women seen on the homepage? A short, tight little black dress.

But, as in the 90s, the LBD can provide its wearer with a seriousness along with sexiness. After the Harvey Weinstein revelations at the end of 2017, actors on the red carpet for the Golden Globes in 2018 used black dresses not as glamour, but as protest. In contrast to the usual rainbow of brights and pastels, black dresses dominated. Part of the Time's Up campaign, A-listers like Reese Witherspoon, Issa Rae, Natalie Portman and Meryl Streep wore black, and were accompanied by feminist activists including Ai-jen Poo and Mónica Ramírez, also in black. "I am wearing black to stand in solidarity with all of the women who have come out about being sexually harassed and abused," said Alison Brie. Black here was a way to draw a line in the sand, to sartorially say Time's Up. The hashtag #whywewearblack has now been used over 37,000 times on Instagram. Activism and LBDs have also been combined on the red carpet to push against gender conformity. See Billy Porter at the 2019 Oscars in a tuxedo-gown with a bustle skirt Anna Karenina would have been proud of.

In 2020, the LBD was employed as a device to speak about seduction, power and sexual violence. In the last episode of Michaela Coel's mind-bending revenge comedy-drama *I May Destroy You*, Coel's character is allowed a fantasy that involves seducing and then violently killing her rapist. She does so while wearing a black rubber LBD and bovver boots, turning from a male fantasy into a pure

A ballgown Anna Karenina would be proud of:
Billy Porter wears a not-so-little black dress to the 2019
Academy Awards

expression of anger. This was a new kind of revenge dress, and yet another interpretation of a forever-changing classic. Because, as it was for Anna Karenina in 1878, the LBD is still a frame. What's in the picture is always up to you.

Maude Bass-Krueger
Historian of visual and material culture

**Maude Bass-Krueger has an impressive CV. Her email
signature states her role as a professor in the Faculty of
Arts and Philosophy at the University of Ghent, and she
has worked on exhibitions, books, several research projects
and articles for *Vogue*. Not only does Bass-Krueger have a
formidable-on-paper profile, she also has serious style.
When I lay eyes on her, I find a young, smiley woman, with a
kind of deconstructed Flock of Seagulls hairdo, and
black and white spotty blouse.**

Of course, the professor seriously knows her stuff – particularly
when it comes to the little black dress, and the role of black in the
mourning practices. She researched it extensively for her 2019 book,
French Fashion, Women & the First World War, co-authored with Sophie
Kurkdjian, which details mourning practices and the kind of "damned
if you do, damned if you don't" attitude from French society towards
widows. "There was great fear of the power that women were gaining
in society," says Bass-Krueger. "So anything that men could use to
dampen women's voices and power in society was used. Mourning
was one such way." But mourning was also heartfelt for these women.
"They were just rather sad biographies of loss," she says of the
mourning dresses from the period.

Pre-war mourning practices, Bass-Krueger says, would broadly
have been three periods: full mourning, second mourning and half-
mourning, each lasting for between three and six months, with different
dress codes and rules applied to each stage, depending on whom you
were mourning. Fashion magazines would devote columns to mourning

fashions. This all increased as the casualties mounted during the war. "A huge part of mourning was being fashionable," says Bass-Krueger. "It was about showing your mourning, but also half about showing that you knew the social conventions." While this was largely only expected of the upper classes, not conforming would have had grave consequences for this demographic. "It would have been *scandalous*," says Bass-Krueger, conspiratorially.

The professor explains that while black was associated with mourning during this period, additional layers of meaning led to a quality we understand: that of seduction. "The shopkeeper's uniform was a black dress," she says. "And shopkeepers, like women who worked in couture workshops, were considered somewhat to be prostitutes as well." So, while the pressure to adhere to mourning codes was a way of patriarchal society dampening down a woman's progress, wearing a black dress also nodded to a sort of sexual availability.

Bass-Krueger, like most fashion historians, is clear that Chanel did not invent the little black dress. "Chanel was a very good marketer," she says. "If you look at the fashion magazines of the time, Chanel has black dresses, but so does Lanvin. So does Weeks." Chanel's minimal take on the item gave her an advantage across the Atlantic, though. "Her silhouettes were widely acclaimed by the American fashion press," says Bass-Krueger. "Americans liked what Chanel was doing. I mean, it was kind of an American style."

Bass-Krueger says mourning practices continued in France into the 50s when, "At the same time that you have a young generation wearing the little black dress out to dance, you still have the grandmothers who would never dream of wearing a black dress outside of mourning."

Now we now wear black dresses for going out clubbing, for a funeral, a black-tie event and the office. And, of course, to give a good impression. Bass-Krueger is no exception. "If I go for a job interview," she says. "I wear a little black dress."

HOW TO WEAR THE LBD NOW

Think about it as something everyday
This will add a sense of casual "no big deal"-ness to proceedings, which the LBD can do with in the twenty-first century. Accessories to consider include trainers, DMs, a hoodie or maybe an oversized trench to add a *soupçon* of insouciance.

Have a few to choose from
The LBD is an adaptable item – it can be sexy, work-appropriate or sober seriousness. But sometimes one dress can't do all of those things. Have a wardrobe of LBDs to be prepared for every occasion, from a night out to a Zoom meeting, or even the weekly shop.

Don't see it as boring
Black is background, yes, but it's also the colour of chic, the colour of rebellion. Embrace those qualities – whichever one appeals to you. That is how you'll find an LBD that pops when you put it on.

Jewellery is your friend
As the likes of Audrey Hepburn in *Breakfast at Tiffany's* and Princess Diana in 1994 attest, black looks great with sparkles. This is not a time to go for subtle – go big or go home. Sunglasses also benefit from this rule of thumb.

Try to avoid wearing with other black items
This can look a bit commuter-on-the-way-home. Black looks great with other colours. Think Saint Laurent and pair it with jewel colours – fuchsia, violet or jade. Add hints of gold to look really glam and expensive.

NEED TO KNOW

- The Little Black Dress is often dated back to October 1926, and Coco Chanel. Her LBD was featured in American *Vogue*, who dubbed it the "Ford" dress, a nod to Henry Ford. The magazine wrote that dresses like this would "become sort of a uniform for all women of taste".

- Something similar had been worn for several decades by this point, mostly by young working-class women in service and shops. This wasn't the LBD as a sign of glamour. It was about making sure these young women didn't threaten the style superiority of the upper classes. Black, at this point, was dowdy and funereal.

- While the LBD has been a staple since the 40s, the colour has been worn as a fashion statement for centuries. Philip the Good, Duke of Burgundy from 1419, was a pioneer. He wore the colour to distinguish himself from his brightly coloured court, and also to mourn his father, who had been assassinated.

- The 80s was a key decade for black. It was worn as a sexy bodycon style, in sculptural shapes by rich bohemians when designed by Rei Kawakubo, and by goths in clubs like London's Batcave. Goths continue to paint it black – the subculture is spotted all over the world and on subreddits.

- Black dresses can now be sexy, but they can also be serious. See the post-Weinstein Golden Globes red carpet, where the Time's Up campaign had A-listers like Issa Rae and Alison Brie wearing black to, as Brie said, "stand in solidarity with all of the women who have come out about being sexually harassed and abused".

THE TRENCH

In Milan in February 2020, I sat waiting for the
Bottega Veneta show to start when, suddenly, the
room hushed – and Sigourney actual Weaver sat
down, next to Dev Hynes and Tessa Thompson.
Once I'd retrieved my jaw from the floor, I idly
noticed she was wearing a trench coat. Then
I noticed that so were Hynes and Thompson,
and – in fact – so were lots of the people like
me, the ones there to work. No, it wasn't raining
that day. Instead, this was a sign the trench was
indisputably a staple of fashionable dressing in
our modern era. Again. As a *Racked* headline put it
in 2017: "This Coat Never Goes Out of Style but
Really We Mean Never."

*In action: Captain Bernard Montgomery and a fellow
soldier wearing trench coats in the First World War*

A COAT FOR ALL SEASONS

THE TRENCH ISN'T THE only item of civilian clothing to come
from the military – there's also the wellington boot, the blazer and even
the wristwatch – but it may be the only one whose name still divulges
its army origins to a modern audience.[1] As it suggests, the coat was
worn in the trenches in the First World War. But, unlike those other
items, the design predates its purpose during war. Its roots are British
– this is, after all, a land where "all the seasons in one day" is a regular
meteorological occurrence. Charles Macintosh, a Scottish chemist, first
popularized waterproofing. He experimented with dissolving rubber and
sandwiching it between two layers of fabric. Patenting this idea in 1823,
he began to make coats, opening a factory in Manchester in 1824.

Mackintosh the brand still exists, selling very expensive, elegantly
functional rainwear – but it wasn't exactly in demand by the smartly

dressed at first. Macks, as they came to be known, were not breathable and gave off a rubbery smell when warm. In 1836, the *Gentleman's Magazine of Fashion* gave a damning verdict: "No one can look like a gentleman in such a garb and it is of a most unpleasant odour."[2]

Macintosh and his partner, Thomas Hancock, sorted out the design flaws, and gentlemen began to buy Macks. Others started to see the potential of rainwear for the well-heeled. John Emary set up his company Aquascutum – Latin for "water shield" – in London in 1851. Two years later, the brand created what they call "the first waterproof wool", and it was used by the British army in the Crimean War. The Latin name, though, was chosen "to reflect its focus on designing wet weather gear for the gentry," wrote Linda Rodriguez McRobbie for the *Smithsonian* magazine. "[Emary's] 'Wrappers' were soon necessities for the well-dressed man who wanted to remain well-dressed in inclement weather."

Thomas Burberry, a 21-year-old draper's apprentice in Basingstoke, set up his eponymous company – or Burberry's, as it was then known – in 1856. It was, as the brand's website puts it, "founded on the principle that clothing should be designed to protect people from the British weather". Burberry invented gabardine in 1879. Studying the lanolin-coated smocks worn by shepherds, he coated individual strands of cotton and wool in a waterproof solution, rather than the fabric as a whole. Breathable and lighter, by the beginning of the twentieth century the fabric was being worn by adventurers like Ernest Shackleton and balloonist Edward Maitland, those who indulged in country pursuits, and officers in the Boer War.

Aquascutum, meanwhile, had the unlikely combination of both the Prince of Wales and the suffragettes as clientele. The company received a royal warrant in 1897, and in 1900 introduced women's coats. Weatherproof and practical shapes made them a hit with the women's movement, keeping protesters warm and dry through marches on the streets of London.

OUTERWEAR GOES TO WAR

IN JULY 1914, the First World War broke out. Due to developments in military technology including an increasing number of machine guns and artillery like the French 75, being a soldier visible to the enemy could result in death or horrific injuries. The trenches dug from September 1914 by opposing sides on the Western Front – running through France, Belgium and Germany – meant both sides largely remained concealed, with the occasional terrifying moment "going over the top". By the end of the war, the system of these muddy, cold, rat-infested trenches would stretch 35,000 miles.

Those in the trenches began to wear trench coats in the first two years of the war. Compared to the greatcoat, the trench was shorter and lighter, with the design allowing ease of movement. It was also more rainproof – essential in the slippery, wet environment of the trench – with a cape across the shoulders and straps around the wrist to prevent water coming in.

The colour of the trench coat, khaki, has its roots in combat too. We now assume that camouflage is advantageous, but battles were waged in bright colours right into the 1870s, as a way to distinguish who was on which side. Khaki – an Urdu word for "dusty" – dates back to the British occupation of India, in what is now Pakistan. The story goes that Sir Harry Lumsden, in 1846 in Peshawar, wanted to make his regiment "invisible in the land of dust", so he bought white cotton and rubbed it with the mud from the local river.[3] Khaki was further adopted by the British army during the Indian Mutiny in 1857. By the twentieth century it was commonplace for British troops.

Aquascutum and Burberry both claim to have made the first trench coat. Aquascutum say they were the first company to outfit the British army in waterproofs, for the Crimean War in the 1850s, while Burberry were commissioned by the British War Office to design a lightweight raincoat in 1900. Burberry's Tielocken design was patented in 1912 and has several of the features we recognize: the double-breasted style, the lapels and the belt at the waist. The coat also had a notable endorsement. It was, as Burberry proclaimed in an advert, "Selected by Lord Kitchener as the most serviceable weather-resistant campaigning coat."

Though the story of the trench has been constructed around the military heroism of the First World War, it was actually only worn by a privileged few – the upper-class officers who bought them at military outfitters like Aquascutum and Burberry. Unlike the private in his issued kit, officers were permitted to have personal style and encouraged to look smart. They were the well-kempt face of the army, the men who stood for discipline and a morale-boosting sense of pride in representing one's country. The trench coat helped officers look the part – and epaulettes let them display their rank for all to see.

By Christmas 1914, more officers were dying than soldiers from the lower ranks. This forced the army to recruit officers where they hadn't before: from the middle- and even working classes. The new recruits, dubbed "temporary gentlemen", may well have used their allowance to buy a trench coat in an effort to blend in with their upper-class colleagues. But, although these temporary gentlemen might have appreciated the trench coat's association with the well-heeled, it was a different quality that made it so highly prized in the trenches: respite from the elements.

The name was set in 1916. Burberry used "trench warm" in adverts, and the term "trench coat" appeared in a trade publication. In 1917, both Aquascutum and Burberry were advertising coats "ready for immediate wear", and Americans were wearing them when they joined the Allied forces that year. By the last year of the war, Burberry were selling the coats to British and American troops from Paris. In the end, the company supplied around half a million coats during the war.

Soldiers weren't the only ones buying trenches. Both Aquascutum and Burberry – and, likely, other brands – originally created their designs for civilians and continued to sell on the home front through the war. An Aquascutum ad from the time is divided into two sections: one aimed at those in the military, for "coats upon which they can place the utmost reliance", another for "ladies and gentlemen".

"A slightly dubious reputation"

THE FIRST WORLD WAR was responsible for 900,000 deaths in the British forces (which included soldiers from countries in the British Empire), with more than two million coming home wounded. Still, in this obliterated society, the longevity and reliability of the trench coat meant they stuck around after the war was over. Writing in *The Trench Book*, Nick Foulkes explains that they "proved almost indestructible. Customers used their coats for decades and fully expected their coats to outlive them, intending to pass them on to future generations."[4]

By the 1930s, the elegant practicality of the trench began to appeal to women. This was possibly down to the fact that they were increasingly venturing outside of the home, so an all-weather item of clothing felt modern, and there was a shift in fashion back to the waist after the flapper. Burberry, Mackintosh and more produced glossy ads, courting the female market, while women like Katharine Hepburn, Marlene Dietrich and Joan Crawford wore them on film.

The rise of hard-boiled fiction – with writers like Raymond Chandler, former PI Dashiell Hammett and Carroll John Daly – signified the trench's first steps towards an association we still know well: that with the detective. As seen on covers of magazines, these characters wore trench coats and were usually accompanied by a woman scantily clad and in distress.

You must remember this: Humphrey Bogart, a giant of gumshoe dressing, wearing requisite crumpled trench

When the hard-boiled detective went from news-stand pulp fiction to cinema screen in the 40s, the trench coat came along. This is where the alliance with the detective was properly cemented. Humphrey Bogart was the ideal – as Sam Spade in *The Maltese Falcon* in 1941, in 1942's *Casablanca* and 1946's *The Big Sleep*. The maverick trench was worn by journalists too – after all, writes Foulkes, "both professions enjoy a slightly dubious reputation."[5] This archetype is now so clichéd that it has become comedy. Characters range from Peter Sellers's Inspector Clouseau to one of my personal trench style icons, Kermit the Frog as a roving news reporter.

At the same time that Bogart was smouldering as Sam Spade, war had once again broken out in real life. With aerial warfare now a given – and trenches less the focus of fighting – the trench coat was less relevant in the Second World War, with shorter styles like the flying jackets used. However, it did have its place. Aquascutum supplied the Allied forces with trench coats. Hitler and the Nazi party also had a fondness for them, with black leather ones worn by the Gestapo. Perhaps it's the benefit of hindsight – or the depiction through 70 years of war movies – but they seem to visually signpost menace.

Respectable types – and outsiders too

THE 50S SAW THE trench for men become the hallmark of respectability, a symbol that the man wearing it was successful and morally upstanding. Rainwear was by this point a developed clothing category for the middle and upper classes in the UK, with the established brands and also Baracuta, founded in Manchester in 1937. Now more famous for the Harrington jacket, their Topliner trench was released in 1949, and targeted men who wanted to give a good impression from home to office door. "There goes a well-dressed man!" proclaimed one ad.[6]

The 50s fashion for a cinched-in waist played to the trench's advantage with women. The cinema again was key here – and again began with images of women in war. Marlene Dietrich in *A Foreign Affair* in 1948, despite playing essentially a Nazi sympathizer, became a trench coat trailblazer. Ingrid Bergman, as a refugee in Paris the same year in *Arch of Triumph*, wears one with a beret. The war movies trailed off, but the trench remained as a symbol of chic. Audrey Hepburn, from *Funny Face* on, was the poster girl. Nancy MacDonell Smith describes her as providing "a convenient shorthand for identifying off-beat female characters", particularly while wearing a trench.[7] The defiantly nonconformist Holly Golightly in *Breakfast at Tiffany's* is the peak of this idea. The scene with her searching for her cat, Cat, in a downpour, has become *the* mid-century trench moment. It's certainly one that I, along with probably thousands of other women, hopelessly attempt to channel every time I put one on.

By the 60s, the association between rainwear and Britain was – no pun intended – entrenched and profitable. Burberry claim that one in five coats exported from the UK in 1965 was made by them. But the trench's connection with French style, beyond Inspector

Raining cats: Audrey Hepburn demonstrating her ability to make the trench look great – even in a downpour

Clouseau, began then too. Yves Saint Laurent adopted the trench from 1962, shortening the design and rendering it in black PVC. It was this so-called *ciré noir* that Catherine Deneuve wore as high-class sex worker Séverine in *Belle de Jour* in 1967. Alicia Drake, in *The Beautiful Fall*, describes the look as pitching "subversive chic against frigid conservatism with devastating success."[8]

William S Burroughs walked this line too. The writer wore the clothes of a businessman, trench coat included, while writing some of the twentieth century's most experimental fiction, maintaining a heroin addiction, living as a gay man and accidentally shooting his wife in a drinking game in 1951. "To keep suspicion at bay, he looked conversely straightedge, nerdy and conformist," writes Terry Newman. "A total disguise to let his imagination do the wandering."[9] John Waters, a teenager in the 60s, says Burroughs was a formative influence. Newman quotes the film-maker talking about Burroughs in 2013: "He was gay and a junkie and he didn't look the parts ... As a young gay man I thought, '*Finally*, a gay man who isn't square.'"[10]

SUPERFLY STYLE

THE BLAXPLOITATION MOVIES of the 70s saw the trench reach another demographic. Films like *Black Caesar*, *Super Fly*, *Shaft*, *Coffy*, *Slaughter's Big Rip-Off*, *Foxy Brown* and *Trouble Man* had Black heroes and heroines, and majority-Black casts, for the first time. They were soundtracked by Black musicians at their peak: James Brown, Isaac Hayes, Marvin Gaye and Curtis Mayfield.

With storylines around crime, Blaxploitation films featured trench coats as part of the look, fitting into the lineage of the detectives on screen stretching back 40 years while – in optics at least – disrupting the white supremacy that assumes all male detectives look like Bogie.

An icon on a classic: the trench as seen on Marvin Gaye's seminal 1971 album, What's Going On

A tan leather trench was worn by Richard Roundtree as detective John Shaft, and Ron O'Neal as Youngblood Priest in *Super Fly* wears a similar design, in what looks like suedette. Those on soundtrack duty wore them too: James Brown on the front of the soundtrack for *Slaughter's Big Rip-Off* wears a black leather trench accessorized with a machine gun, and both Mayfield and Hayes were fond of them. The year before *Trouble Man*, the cover of Gaye's now classic 1971 album *What's Going On* featured him in a black PVC trench coat.

Blaxploitation films have been questioned almost from the get-go. Critics in the Black community observed how their Black characters were often stereotyped as criminal and sexual, but also how – even with Black actors and directors – the strings were pulled by white people, often writing and producing the films. Despite these undeniable issues, "the era still represents one of the most sustained periods of cinema featuring Black themes and Black performers of any in film history," wrote academic Dr Todd Boyd in *The Guardian* in 2018. He argues the films were "uniquely adept at capturing the cultural zeitgeist in a period of a newly free sense of Black identity."

Blaxploitation films were popular: 1971's *Shaft*, directed by Gordon Parks, one of the few Black directors working on these films, was the biggest hit: it topped the box office for five weeks, and was the 14th highest grossing movie of the year. Roundtree's look was part of the film's success – there was even a *Shaft* clothing line. Speaking in 2019, costume designer Joe Aulisi said the idea of the trench came from Parks, because he thought it would look good on film. He was right.

DRESSING FOR SUCCESS

IF BLAXPLOITATION FAVOURED a statement take on the trench coat, the more familiar khaki model – particularly by Burberry, and particularly in the US – became a core component of the white-collar wardrobe, worn by both genders to get ahead. Both Dustin Hoffman and Meryl Streep, playing middle-class New Yorkers, wear them in 1979's *Kramer vs. Kramer*. A scene between Hoffman and his boss is revealing, with Hoffman arguing that in order to wear success, "You need to get yourself a Burberry trench coat."

This was certainly the case in the 1980s when yuppie culture properly hit. A term first used in 1980 as a catch-all for young urban professionals, four years later *Newsweek* was declaring 1984 "the year of the yuppie", pinning their cover story to the estimated four million 25–39-year-olds earning more than $40,000 a year (over $100,000 in today's money). The trench coat was, as Hoffman's character suggested, a trope of their success. Michael Douglas wears a trench as Gordon

Dressing for success: the trench was the yuppie coat of choice, as modelled by Meryl Streep in Kramer vs. Kramer

Gekko in 1987's *Wall Street*. In *Working Girl*, Tess McGill switches from leather jacket to trench coat, as a sign of going up in the world. Foulkes sees this as harking back to the trench coat's purpose in warfare: "The wearer, consciously or subconsciously, hopes that a little of the captain – captain of industry, that is – will rub off on him."[11] Or, indeed, her.

Style – and subversion

AS THE TRENCH BECAME the symbol of the yuppie, it was also worn, perhaps with a dash of irony, by those who were anything but. Sid Vicious wore a trench coat, as did Patti Smith. Ian Curtis, the frontman of Joy Division, wore the clothes of his previous life as a civil servant – including a grey trench coat – but wrote songs of existential bleakness. As *AnOther Magazine* suggested in 2019: "Beneath the measured exterior – beneath that stark, utilitarian uniform – was something else, intoxicating and violent, waiting to escape." It struck a chord with other young people processing the futility of life. They began to dress like their idol. Music journalist Simon Reynolds writes of an "increasingly obsessive following, nicknamed the 'Cult with no Name' and, according to stereotype, consisting of intense young men dressed in grey overcoats."[12] When Curtis committed suicide in 1980, the cult's fanatical nature only grew.

And then there is Prince in 1980, on the cover of third album *Dirty Mind*, dressed in an open trench coat, skimpy black underwear, thigh-high stockings and heeled boots – the furthest away from the office-ready trench you could get. In videos, he spun around in it coquettishly, in a way more typically seen by a young woman in a flared skirt. As a bit of a Prince head, this may be my favourite trench moment ever.

Talking to Chris Salewicz for *NME* in 1981, Prince asserts the trench is "the only coat I've got". But don't be fooled – the singer knew

*Baby, he's a star: Prince's trench, worn in 1981 with
stockings and suspenders, was anything but respectable.
That's why it was genius*

the importance of image. In the – pun intended this time – purple patch of the first half of the 80s, Prince's sound evolved, but the trademark studded trench remained in one form or another: it was black for the "Controversy" video, sparkly for "1999", and finally, purple taffeta for *Purple Rain*. "I chose this fabric because it was attention-grabbing," said costume designer Louis Wells to *Billboard* in 2016. "And a trench because he loved the drama and fit. You never knew what it would reveal when it blew open." If yuppies wore the trench to go to battle on a work day, Prince recognized, and played with, the erotic suggestion of the wrap-around design, and the frisson that came from the fact this was a truly gender-neutral item, one imbued with sex appeal when worn by a woman. As MacDonell Smith writes: "Black lace bras and garters have nothing on a tightly cinched trench."[13]

To this day, Prince's *Dirty Mind* trench remains a subversive, groundbreaking and nuanced image of male sexuality. One that Frank Ocean paid tribute to on his Tumblr when Prince died in 2016: "He was a straight Black man who played his first televised set in bikini bottoms and knee-high heeled boots, epic," he wrote. "He made me feel more comfortable with how I identify sexually simply by his display of freedom from and irreverence for obviously archaic ideas like gender conformity etc." Contemporary reactions reveal how much of a disruptor he was. "We didn't know what the fuck Prince was," Ice-T told Alan Light for his book *Let's Go Crazy*. "Prince is dope, he's a motherfucker, but he was really hard to figure out."[14] A more aggressive reaction occurred in 1981 when Prince and his band opened for The Rolling Stones in his trench and pants. Pelted with food and racist and homophobic slurs, the performance lasted five minutes. Wendy Melvoin, a soon-to-be bandmate, put it this way: "This was a serious rock and roll crowd. They didn't want to see a Black guy in a bikini and a trench coat."[15] Fast-forward three years and they had changed their minds – the *Purple Rain* tour sold 1.7 million tickets worldwide.

Sinister, aristo, classic

THE 90S WASN'T EXACTLY a trench desert – but memorable moments were few and far between. It's there on Madonna and Warren Beatty in *Dick Tracy*, Agent Cooper in *Twin Peaks*, the Olsen twins as kiddy PIs, a young Chloë Sevigny. At the end of the decade, things changed. *The Matrix* – now a style reference for Gen Z – was released in 1999 and started a trend for long, black, sometimes leather, sometimes PVC trench coats; even if only one character, Laurence Fishburne's Morpheus, actually wears a trench. The same year, although unconnected, a similar black trench coat became caught up with tragedy. It was worn by Eric Harris and Dylan Klebold, the two teenagers who plotted a shooting at Columbine High School, killing 13 people and themselves. Initially thought to have been in with a social group called "the trench coat mafia", who dressed in long black trenches, various schools banned the item in the months afterwards.

Far away from Columbine, in central London, a plan was developing to make the Burberry trench coat – now seen by luxury customers as mundane at best – fashionable again. In 1997, the ailing company appointed Rose Marie Bravo from Saks, as chief executive. Burberry grew from a value of £200 million to £1.5 billion in 2002. Bravo hired Kate Moss for an ad campaign and rebranded from Burberry's to Burberry, with a new Fabien Baron logo. She brought the brand's check back, on everything from trench coats to bikinis, and, in 2001, announced Christopher Bailey, then at Gucci, as design director.

Bailey, a Yorkshire lad very familiar with the ways of the British weather, took the trench from the commute and put it on the catwalk, and on young aristo types in ad campaigns. Bravo's reintroduction of check coincided with a logomania moment in fashion, and young working-class people – dubbed "chavs" and often mocked and vilified – wore the pattern. The association was judged unseemly for a luxury brand. Consequently, the check was reduced, and the trench became the rebooted brand's calling card. Foregrounding Burberry's well-heeled heritage, it projected what *The Guardian* called "an RP kind of Britishness".

Even beyond Burberry, the RP trench dominated for over a decade. It was Kate Middleton, buttoned up and all smart. It was Kerry Washington's Olivia Pope getting things handled in *Scandal*. It was Olivia Palermo doing her best Audrey Hepburn impression. It was also, as Linda Grant writes, the item appropriate for people of a certain age – along with the white shirt and low-heeled shoes, "those styles despondently known as classic".[16]

That changed sometime around late 2016, when Kim Kardashian was photographed at a fashion show in an outfit Prince might have approved of: a trench coat and thigh-high boots, cleavage on display. By the following summer, the trench had been spotted on the catwalk beyond Burberry, at Vetements and Phoebe Philo's Céline. Clever young people, realizing this was a pretty easy look to replicate, borrowed their parents' trenches, or bought one on eBay. And crucially, they didn't do a Kate Middleton – they wore their trenches open, with nonchalance and a ‾_(ツ)_/‾, like celebrities including Gigi Hadid and Rihanna.

This trend happily coincided with a new appointment at Burberry – Bailey was out and Riccardo Tisci, the man who brought hoodies and sneakers to Givenchy, was in. His first collection for Burberry featured 20 trench coats. In 2019, he told me he appreciates the way they denote success in British society. With the romance of a creative type, Tisci ignores the class nuances – he reads the trench coat as every-item in British culture. "When you behave well at school, in France you get the Chanel bag," he said. "In England, you get the Burberry trench." Make no mistake, the £1,500 Burberry trench – much like the Chanel bag – is not a regular purchase for a family of average means.

Of course, the trench is now widely available – you can spend much less than the price of a Burberry, and much, much more. Its position in fashion is solid. Meghan Markle wore one to announce her engagement to Prince Harry in 2017, Arsenal player Héctor Bellerín wore one to announce his general fashion prowess in 2019. And there's Sigourney and friends at the Bottega Veneta show – the ones who convinced me dig out my trench coat, to style it open and add a bit of a twirl. I'm not quite as brave as Prince, but I like to think I pay tribute to him just a little bit every time I wear it.

The trench, front row: on Sigourney Weaver, Dev Hynes
and Tessa Thompson at the Bottega Veneta show

HOW TO WEAR
THE TRENCH NOW

Keep it open
We're not in a moment where smartness equals style. Wearing a trench open means you get an edge of nonchalance that chimes with the zeitgeist. As seen on street-style blogs and, well, the street for the past few years.

Try a *ciré noir*
Saint Laurent's one for Catherine Deneuve serves as inspiration, or Marvin Gaye's PVC on the front of *What's Going On*. Either way, the shininess of the fabric crashes into the military shape of the trench in an extremely appealing way.

"Irreverence" is a key adjective
In the past, the trench would have been worn over office-ready clothes. But to keep it updated is to keep it casual.

Jeans and trainers are a sort of "up-yours" to convention – and they're much more comfortable too.

Go beyond khaki
A coloured trench is a way to wear the classic, while also pushing things a bit further. Think pink, green or bright red. Ochre, rust, grey and navy blue don't count as experimenting, sorry.

Wear with your own take
Meghan Markle's polished trench-dress. Kim Kardashian's trench-corset. Héctor Bellerín's nod to terrace style while watching a game from the terraces during an injury spell... The best way to wear a trench – such an item of anonymity – is by adding a hefty dose of you.

NEED TO KNOW

- The first trench pre-dates the First World War. Styles were produced by both Aquascutum and Burberry from the mid-nineteenth century onwards. Burberry's Tielocken, patented in 1912, has recognizable trench traits – including the double-breasted style, the lapels and the belt at the waist. In the war, the item signalled a hierarchy – it was worn by only officers, not all soldiers.

- Rainwear, meanwhile, dates back to 1823, and Charles Macintosh, who made the rubber-based waterproofs later known as Macks. Aquascutum – Latin for "water shield" – followed in 1851, and created so-called "waterproof wool". Thomas Burberry founded his company aged 21, in 1856. In 1879, he invented gabardine, the breathable and lighter waterproof fabric still used today.

- The detective is the classic trench wearer. This archetype goes back to the 1930s – and hard-boiled fiction. On the covers of pulp magazines, they wore trench coats and were usually accompanied by a woman scantily clad and in distress. Humphrey Bogart as Sam Spade in *The Maltese Falcon* and, later, Richard Roundtree in *Shaft* brought the look to the cinema.

- The trench was a yuppie favourite, worn by *Working Girl*'s Tess McGill when she moves up the ladder, and both Kramers in *Kramer vs. Kramer*. But it's also a trope of outsider figures from William S Burroughs to Ian Curtis. After all, there is little the counterculture likes more than subverting the codes of mainstream society.

- Christopher Bailey at Burberry can be credited with putting the trench back on the fashion agenda. Appointed in 2001, he used the trench as Burberry's new calling card. It projected what *The Guardian* called "an RP kind of Britishness".

Laura Clouting
Senior curator historian,
Imperial War Museum

**Laura Clouting is not a woman to mince her words.
Asked who she believes the trench was invented by –
Aquascutum or Burberry – she replies: "I mean, to be
brutally honest, to me that is an irrelevance.
The application of this item of clothing in the
First World War is where my interest is piqued."**

Indeed. Clouting, who – rightly for someone so learned – sits in an impressively book- and box file-lined office, is determined to take the story of the trench coat away from conjecture and back to the historical reality of the First World War. She says the biggest myth is that all soldiers wore trench coats, as opposed to just officers: "People have built up the idea that everyone who was in a trench wore one," she says. This is part of a bigger misconception. "Any time we think of the First World War, we think of trenches," says Clouting "but [soldiers] were out in Mesopotamia and Salonica in the boiling heat and they were wearing completely different types of uniform and suffering malaria and flies … [the trench is a] very dominant experience, but it is by no means the only one."

In the trenches, the design that would become known as the trench coat took off not because of style, but because of its sheer practicality. It was this factor, in this environment, that made it a desirable item. "Those are the kind of things [mentioned] in adverts as in those by Burberry," she says. "'So-and-so in the army has had his for eight months and it's keeping the rain off nicely' … People of means are being advertised to accordingly."

The First World War inadvertently became something of a shop window for brands like Burberry and Aquascutum to demonstrate the durability of their designs. "It's an opportunity, isn't it?" says Clouting. "You've got this technology you have created to keep the rain off you, it already exists, produce it en masse and get more and more people wearing it, because they are in a situation where actually it's incredibly useful." The war, and its unprecedented global nature, put more eyes on this design than ever before. "Had the war not turned into such a massive endeavour, you wouldn't have had so many people wearing the trench coat," says Clouting.

The curator, who is wearing a very nice blouse with a floral print that could have been found on a 40s tea dress, does not own a trench coat herself. But she recognizes it is a style loved by the fashion crowd. "The attraction for us to this military-inspired clothing is something about simplicity, not being very garnished with fripperies," she says. But even the straight-talking Clouting admits there is more to clothes than protecting ourselves from the elements. She says emotions came into play, with those in the army continuing to wear their trench coats after the war. "For a lot of people it was a very meaningful experience, it might not have been all awful, they might have thought about the camaraderie and that sort of thing," she says. "I think with any item of clothing that survived the war, it's about the memories imbued in that clothing."

Symbolism still plays a part today. "We have come to associate it with competence or at least control," says Clouting. "The people that wear these are leaders. Even if we don't wear one ourselves we might think [someone in a trench] looks very suave, like they know what they're doing." And that, of course, is an appealing idea to everyone with a touch of imposter syndrome: from a new officer in the First World War to a new fashion editor making their way in the front row, 100 years later.

FOOTNOTES

INTRODUCTION

1. Lurie, Alison. 1981. *The Language of Clothes*. London: Random House, p.4.

THE WHITE T-SHIRT

1. Adlington, Lucy. 2016. *Stitches in Time: The Story of the Clothes We Wear*. London: Random House, p.24.
2. Antonelli, Paola and Millar Fisher, Michelle, eds. 2017. *Items: Is Fashion Modern?* New York: The Museum of Modern Art, p.263.
3. Steele, Valerie, ed. 2010.*The Berg Companion to Fashion*. New York: Berg Publishers, p.691.
4. Ibid., p.691
5. Ibid., p.691
6. Gunn, Tim with Calhoun, Ada. 2012. *Tim Gunn's Fashion Bible: A Fascinating History of Everything in Your Closet*. New York: Gallery Books, p.27.
7. Easby, Amber and Oliver, Henry. 2007. *The Art of the Band T-shirt*. New York: Pocket Books, p.2
8. Steele, Op. cit., p.691.
9. Ibid., p.691.
10. Antonelli and Fisher, Op. cit., p.263.
11. Gunn with Calhoun, Op. cit., p.27.
12. Steele, Op. cit., p.692.
13. Antonelli and Fisher, Op. cit., p.131.
14. Easby and Oliver, Op. cit., p.14.
15. Ibid., p.3.
16. Antonelli and Fisher, Op. cit., p.130.
17. Steele, Op. cit., p.692.
18. Newman, Terry. 2017. *Legendary Authors and the Clothes They Wore*. New York: Harper Design, p.95.
19. Ibid., p.92.
20. Hebdige, Dick. 1979. *Subculture: The Meaning of Style*. Oxford: Routledge, p.107.
21. Gunn with Calhoun, Op. cit., p.30.
22. Steele, Op. cit., p.692.
23. Antonelli and Fisher, Op. cit., p.131.
24. Steele, Op. cit., p.693.
25. Gorman, Paul. 2001. *The Look: Adventures in Rock & Pop Fashion*. New York: Sanctuary Publishing Ltd, p.186.
26. Easby and Oliver, Op. cit., p.6-7.
27. Gunn with Calhoun, Op. cit., p.30.
28. Antonelli and Fisher, Op. cit., p.132.
29. Jaeger, Anne-Celine. 2009. *Fashion Makers, Fashion Shapers: The Essential Guide to Fashion by Those in the Know*. London: Thames & Hudson, p.87.
30. Mackinney-Valentin, Maria. 2017. *Fashioning Identity: Status Ambivalence in Contemporary Fashion*. London: Bloomsbury, p.99.
31. Brooks, Andrew. 2015. *Clothing Poverty, The Hidden World of Fast Fashion and Second-hand Clothes*. London: Zed Books Ltd, p.251.
32. Ibid., p.29.
33. Spivack, Emily. 2017. *Worn in New York: 68 Sartorial Memoirs of the City*. New York: Abrams, p.81.

THE MINISKIRT

1. Levy, Shawn. 2014. *Ready, Steady, Go: Swinging London and the Invention of Cool*. London: Fourth Estate, p.240.
2. Quant, Mary. 2018. *Quant By Quant: The Autobiography of Mary Quant*. London: V&A, p.18.
3. Quant, Op. cit., p.36.
4. Levy, Op. cit., p.54.
5. Sandbrook, Dominic. 2009. *White Heat: A History of Britain in the Swinging Sixties 1964-1970*. London: Abacus, p.453.
6. Levy, Op. cit., p.7.
7. Sandbrook, Op. cit., p.234.
8. Ibid., p.244.
9. Baxter, Mark; Brummell, Jason and Snowball, Ian (eds). 2016. *Ready Steady Girls*. London: Suave Collective Publishing, p. 40.
10. Laver, James. 1969. *A Concise History of Costume*. London: Thames & Hudson, p.259.
11. Bass-Krueger, Maude and Kurkdjian, Sophie eds. 2019. *French Fashion, Women, and the First World War*. New Haven: Yale University Press, p.82.
12. Ibid., p.266
13. Shulman, Alexandra. 2020. *Clothes…and other things that matter*. London: Cassell, p.56.
14. Laver, Op. cit., p.263-4.
15. Levy, Ariel. 2006. *Feminist Chauvinist Pigs: Women and the Rise of Raunch Culture*. London: Simon & Schuster, p.4.

16. Ibid., p.5.
17. Bartley, Luella. 2011. *Luella's Guide to English Style*. London: Fourth Estate, p.250.

THE JEANS
1. Maries, Patrick and Napias, Jean-Christophe. 2016. *Fashion Quotes: Stylish Wit & Catwalk Wisdom*. London: Thames & Hudson, p.118.
2. Sullivan, James. 2006. *Jeans: A Cultural History of an American Icon*. Hollywood: Gotham Books, p.26.
3. Ibid., p.12-13.
4. Gunn, Tim with Calhoun, Ada. 2012. *Tim Gunn's Fashion Bible: A Fascinating History of Everything in Your Closet*. New York: Gallery Books, p.41.
5. St Clair, Kassia. 2018. *The Secret Lives of Colour*. London: John Murray, p.190-1.
6. Adlington, Lucy. 2016. *Stitches in Time: The Story of the Clothes We Wear*. London: Random House, p.167.
7. Sullivan, Op. cit., p.62.
8. Miller, Daniel and Woodward, Sophie, eds. 2010. *Global Denim*. London: Berg Publishers, p.34.
9. Ibid., p.38
10. Tuite, Rebecca C. 2017. *Seven Sisters Style: The All-American Preppy Look*. New York: Universe Publishing, p.43.
11. Polhemus, Ted. 2010. *Street Style*. London: PYMCA, p.24.
12. Sullivan, Op. cit., p.108.
13. Brooks, Andrew. 2015. *Clothing Poverty, The Hidden World of Fast Fashion and Second-hand Clothes*. London: Zed Books Ltd, p.291.
14. Sullivan, Op. cit., p.138.
15. Ibid., p.126-7.
16. Steele, Valerie, ed. 2010.*The Berg Companion to Fashion*. New York: Berg Publishers, p.281.
17. Bernstein, Bill. 2015. *Disco: The Bill Bernstein Photographs*. London: Reel Art Press, p.10.
18. George, Nelson. 2005. *Hip Hop America*. New York: Penguin Books, p.163.
19. Miller and Woodward eds., Op. cit., p.161.
20. Brooks, Op. cit., p.28.
21. Antonelli, Paola and Millar Fisher, Michelle, eds. 2017. *Items: Is Fashion Modern?*. New York: The Museum of Modern Art, p.34.

22. Brooks, Op. cit., p.30.
23. Corner, Frances. 2014. *Why Fashion Matters*. London: Thames & Hudson, p.26.
24. Brooks, Op. cit., p.42.
25. Polhemus, Op. cit., p.24.

THE BALLET FLAT
1. Mears, Patricia et al. 2019. *Ballerina: Fashion's Modern Muse*. New York: Vendome Press, p.7.
2. Ibid., p.191.
3. Ibid., p.177.
4. Antonelli, Paola and Millar Fisher, Michelle, eds. 2017. *Items: Is Fashion Modern?*. New York: The Museum of Modern Art, p.49.
5. Welters, Linda and Cunningham, Patricia A. eds. 2005. *Twentieth Century American Fashion*. London: Bloomsbury, p.156.
6. Mears et al., Op. cit., p.217.
7. Heti, Sheila, Julavits, Heidi, and Shapton, Leanne eds. 2014.*Women In Clothes: Why We Wear What We Wear*. London: Particular Book, p.275.
8. Tolentino, Jia. 2020. *Trick Mirror: Reflections on Self-Delusion*. London: Fourth Estate, p.77.

THE HOODIE
1. Kinney, Alison. 2016. *Hood*. London: Bloomsbury Academic, p.5.
2. Ibid., p.50.
3. Ibid., p.38.
4. Ibid., p.40.
5. Antonelli, Paola and Millar Fisher, Michelle, eds. 2017. *Items: Is Fashion Modern?* New York: The Museum of Modern Art, p.143
6. Jenkins, Sacha. 2015. *Fresh Dressed*. Samuel Goldwyn Films, 17:00.
7. George, Nelson. 2005. *Hip Hop America*. New York: Penguin Books, p.211.

THE BRETON
1. Picardie, Justine. 2017. *Coco Chanel: The Legend and the Life*. London: Harper Collins, p.176.
2. Pastourau, Michel. 2001. *The Devil's Cloth: A History of Stripes and Striped Fabric*. Columbia: Columbia University Press, p.88-89.
3. Steele, Valerie eds. *Paris: Capital of Fashion*.

London: Bloomsbury Visual Arts, p.165,
4. Ibid., p.178.

THE STILETTO

1. Czerwinski, Michael. 2009. *Fifty Shoes that Changed the World*. London: Conran, p.32.
2. Steele, Valerie, ed. 2010.*The Berg Companion to Fashion*. New York: Berg Publishers, p.409.
3. Ibid., p. 637
4. MacDonell Smith, Nancy. 2003. *The Classic Ten: The True Story of the Little Black Dress and Nine Other Fashion Items*. London: Penguin Books, p.115.
5. Brennan, Summer. 2019. *High Heel*. London: Bloomsbury Academic, p.40.
6. Steele, Op. cit., p.409.
7. MacDonell Smith, Op. cit., p.107.
8. Adlington, Lucy. 2016. *Stitches in Time: The Story of the Clothes We Wear*. London: Random House, p.275.
9. Steele, Op. cit., p.634.
10. Ibid., p.408.
11. MacDonell Smith, Op. cit., p.110.
12. Steele, Op. cit., p.409.
13. Ibid., p.409.
14. *High Heel*, p.125.
15. Quick, Harriet. *Vogue: The Shoe*. London: Conran, p.16.
16. Brennan, Op. cit., p.92.
17. Ibid., p.142.
18. Steele, Op. cit., p.186.
19. MacDonell Smith, Op. cit., p.109.
20. Steele, Op. cit., p.332.
21. Brennan, Op. cit., p.49-50.
22. Quick, Op. cit., p.70
23. Pedersen, Stephanie. 2005. *Shoes: What Every Woman Should Know*. Exeter: David & Charles, p. 110.
24. MacDonell Smith, Op. cit., p.103.
25. Pedersen, Op. cit., p.55.
26. Grant, Linda. 2009. *The Thoughtful Dresser*. London: Virago, p.295.
27. Brennan, Op. cit., p.137.
28. Czerwinski, Op. cit., p.78.
29. Quick, Op. cit., p.66.

THE BIKER JACKET

1. Antonelli, Paola and Millar Fisher, Michelle, eds. 2017. *Items: Is Fashion Modern?* New York: The Museum of Modern Art p.57.

2. Ibid., p.57.
3. Farren, Mick. 1985. *The Black Leather Jacket*. London: Plexus Publishing Limited. p.32-33.
4. Ibid., p.25.
5. Sullivan, James. 2006. *Jeans: A Cultural History of an American Icon*. Hollywood: Gotham Books, p.91.
6. Antonelli and Millar Fisher, Op. cit., p.57.
7. Sullivan, Op. cit., p.90.
8. Ibid., p.90-1
9. Antonelli and Millar Fisher, Op. cit., p.57.
10. Ibid., p.57.
11. Polhemus, Ted. 2010. *Street Style*. London: PYMCA, p.27.
12. Ibid., p.46.
13. Ibid., p.46.
14. Ibid., p.47.
15. Ibid., p.47.
16. Sandbrook, Dominic. 2009. *White Heat: A History of Britain in the Swinging Sixties 1964-1970*. London: Abacus, p.208.
17. Ibid., p.207.
18. Drake, Alicia. 2007. *The Beautiful Fall: Fashion, Genius and Glorious Excess in 1970s Paris*. London: Bloomsbury, p.29.
19. Yates, Richard. 2008. *The Easter Parade*. London: Vintage Classics, p.183.
20. Reynolds, Simon. 2012. *Retromania: Pop Culture's Addiction to its Own Past*. London: Faber & Faber, p.305.
21. Ibid., p.306-7
22. Farren, Op. cit., p.103.
23. Spivack, Emily. 2017. *Worn in New York: 68 Sartorial Memoirs of the City*. New York: Abrams, p.61
24. Antonelli and Millar Fisher, Op. cit., p.58.
25. Farren, Op. cit., p.102.

THE LBD

1. Bari, Shahidha. 2009. *Dressed: The Secret Life of Clothes*. London: Jonathon Cape, p.77.
2. Ludot, Didier. 2001. *The Little Black Dress*. New York: Assouline Publishing, p.5.
3. Mendes, Valerie D. 1999. *Black in Fashion*, London: V&A Publications, p.29.
4. Steele, Valerie, ed. 2010.*The Berg Companion to Fashion*. New York: Berg Publishers, p. 39.
5. Davis, Fred. 1994. *Fashion, Culture, and Identity*. Chicago: University of Chicago Press. p.57.

6. Picardie, Justine. 2017. *Coco Chanel: The Legend and the Life*. London: Harper Collins, p.58.
7. Bass-Krueger, Maude and Kurkdjian, Sophie eds. 2019. *French Fashion, Women, and the First World War*. New Haven: Yale University Press p.202.
8. Mendes, Op. cit., p.10.
9. Davis, Op. cit., p.64.
10. Antonelli, Paola and Millar Fisher, Michelle, eds. 2017. *Items: Is Fashion Modern?* New York: The Museum of Modern Art, p.163.
11. Ludot, Op. cit., p.8
12. Mendes, Op. cit., introduction.
13. Wilson, Elizabeth. 2009. *Adorned In Dreams*. London: I. B. Tauris & Co. Ltd, p.186.
14. Steele, Op. cit., p.605.
15. Bari, Op. cit., p.263.
16. Ibid., p.263
17. Wilson, Op. cit., p.186.
18. Lurie, Alison. 1992. *The Language of Clothes*. London: Bloomsbury Publishing, p.190.
19. Mendes, Op. cit., p.8.
20. Bass-Krueger and Kurkdjian, Op. cit., p.209.
21. Ibid., p.210.
22. Mendes, Op. cit., p.87.
23. Ibid., p.89.
24. Wilson, Mary with Bego, Mark. 2019. *Supreme Glamour*. London: Thames & Hudson Ltd, p. 84.
25. Mendes, Op. cit., p.17.
26. MacDonell Smith, Nancy. 2003. *The Classic Ten: The True Story of the Little Black Dress and Nine Other Fashion Items*. London: Penguin Books, p.16.
27. Mendes, Op. cit., p.17.
28. Ibid., p.8.
29. Ibid., p.17.

THE TRENCH
1. MacDonell Smith, Nancy. 2003. *The Classic Ten: The True Story of the Little Black Dress and Nine Other Fashion Items*. London: Penguin Books, p.148.
2. Foulkes, Nick. 2007. *The Trench Book*. New York: Assouline Publishing, p.29.
3. St Clair, Kassia. 2018. *The Secret Lives of Colour*. London: John Murray, p.240.
4. Foulkes, Op. cit., p.117.
5. Ibid., p.272.
6. Drake, Alicia. 2007. *The Beautiful Fall: Fashion, Genius and Glorious Excess in 1970s Paris*. London: Bloomsbury, p.8.
7. MacDonell Smith, Op. cit., p.155.
8. Drake, Op. cit., p.49-50.
9. Newman, Terry. 2017. *Legendary Authors and the Clothes They Wore*. New York: Harper Design, p.9.
10. Ibid., p.170.
11. Foulkes, Op. cit., p. 291.
12. Reynolds, Simon. 2019. *Rip It Up and Start Again: Postpunk 1978–1984*. London: Faber & Faber, p.176.
13. MacDonell Smith, Op. cit., p.145.
14. Light, Alan. 2014. *Let's Go Crazy: Prince and the Making of Purple Rain*. New York: Atria Books, p.39.
15. Thorne, Matt. 2013. *Prince*. London: Faber & Faber, p.68.
16. Grant, Linda. 2009. *The Thoughtful Dresser*. London: Virago, p.191.

RESOURCES: WEBSITES

1843 Magazine, www.economist.com
Allure, www.allure.com
Another Magazine, www.anothermag.com
Archive Vintage, archivevintage.com
Business of Fashion, www.businessoffashion.com
Clothes on Film, clothesonfilm.com
Cosmopolitan, www.cosmopolitan.com
CR Fashion Book, www.crfashionbook.com

Dazed Beauty, www.dazeddigital.com
Ethical Gallery, www.ethicalgallery.com.au
Fashionista, fashionista.com/
GQ, www.gq.com
Grazia, graziadaily.co.uk
Harpers Bazaar, www.harpersbazaar.com
i-D Vice, i-d.vice.com
InStyle, www.instyle.com

Interview Magazine, www.interviewmagazine.com
Maire Claire, www.marieclaire.co.uk
MoMA, medium.com/items
Paper Magazine, www.papermag.com
Repeller, repeller.com
Rolling Stone, www.rollingstone.com
Slate, slate.com
Smithsonian Magazine, www.smithsonianmag.com
Textile World, www.textileworld.com
The Atlantic, www.theatlantic.com
The Conversation, theconversation.com

The Fabulous Times, www.thefaboustimes.com
The Guardian, www.theguardian.com
The New York Times, www.nytimes.com
The New Yorker, www.newyorker.com
The Telegraph, fashion.telegraph.co.uk
V&A Museum, www.vam.ac.uk/
Vanity Fair, www.vanityfair.com
Velvet Magazine, velvet-mag.com
Vice, www.vice.com
Vogue, www.vogue.com
Vox, www.vox.com

CREDITS

The publishers would like to thank the following sources for their kind permission to reproduce the pictures in this book.

7. Allen Ginsberg/Corbis via Getty Images, 8. David Montgomery/Getty Images, 10. Ron Galella, Ltd./Ron Galella Collection via Getty Images, 14. Eliot Elisofon/The LIFE Premium Collection via Getty Images/Getty Images, 18. Moviestore/Shutterstock, 21. A Di Crollalanza/Shutterstock, 22. © Liz Cowan, 26. Mario Ruiz/The LIFE Images Collection via Getty Images/Getty Images, 31. Tristan Fewings/BFC/Getty Images for BFC, 38. Popperfoto via Getty Images/Getty Images, 45. Larry Ellis/Express/Getty Images, 46. Bev Grant/Getty Images, 49. Hi-Story/Alamy, 50. Pete Still/Redferns/Getty Images, 53. Richard Young/Shutterstock, 62. ullstein bild/ullstein bild via Getty Images, 66. Private Collection, 69. Fred W. McDarrah/Getty Images, 70. Advertising Archives, 73. CBW/Alamy Stock Photo, 76. KMazur/WireImage/Getty Images, 87. Lebrecht Music Arts/Bridgeman Images, 90. Serge Balkin/Conde Nast via Getty Images, 92. Everett Collection/Alamy Stock Photo, 95. Shutterstock, 100. Courtesy of Cira Robinson, 103. Melodie Jeng/Getty Images, 110. Allison Joyce/Getty Images, 116. Arthur Sidey/Mirrorpix/Getty Images, 119. Moviestore/Shutterstock, 120. Album/Alamy Stock Photo, 125. Ray Tang/Shutterstock, 128. Francois Deshayes/Besti/Sipa/Shutterstock, 134. Granger/Shutterstock, 137. Gaston Paris/Roger Viollet via Getty Images, 140. Hulton Archive/Getty Images,

143. Steve Schapiro/Corbis via Getty Images, 144. Koh Hasebe/Shinko Music/Getty Images, 148. © Sandra Semburg, 153. Max Mumby/Indigo/Getty Images, 158. 20th Century-Fox/Getty Images, 164. Hulton Archive/Getty Images, 166. © Photo by Diana Davies, Manuscripts and Archives Division, The New York Public Library, 169. Landmark Media/Alamy Stock Photo, 172. George Napolitano/FilmMagic/Getty Images, 175. Valery Hache/AFP via Getty Images, 182. Columbia/Kobal/Shutterstock, 188. David Fenton/Getty Images, 191. Shelia Rock/Shutterstock, 192. © Tom of Finland Foundation/Artist Rights Society (ARS), New York/DACS, London 2020, 198. Melodie Jeng/Getty Images, 206. Illustration by Condé Nast via Getty Images, 215. Michael Ochs Archives/Getty Images, 217. PYMCA/Universal Images Group via Getty Images, 220. Dave Benett/Hulton Archive/Getty Images, 223. Frazer Harrison/Getty Images, 230. Imperial War Museums, London (Q 112044), 235. Bettmann/Getty Images, 237. Mondadori via Getty Images, 239. Jan Sandvik Editorial/Alamy Stock Photo, 241. Snap/Shutterstock, 243. Michael Ochs Archives/Getty Images, 247. Jacopo M. Raule/Getty Images for Bottega Veneta

Every effort has been made to acknowledge correctly and contact the source and/or copyright holder of each picture and Welbeck Publishing apologises for any unintentional errors or omissions, which will be corrected in future editions of this book.